Healing Wings

Acts of Jesus for Human Wholeness

ERIC LOTT

Poems by
JANE SAHI

Ink and Pastel drawings by
JYOTI SAHI

ASIAN TRADING CORPORATION
150, Brigade Road, Bangalore 560 025
India

1998

Pub. No. 305

ISBN 81-7086-217-5

Published by Dr. C. C. Pais for Asian Trading Corporation, 150, Brigade Road, Bangalore 560 025. Tel. : 5587807. Fax : 5596363.
Printed at Brilliant Printers, Bangalore 560 054

Dedicated to the Memory of
Shanti Sahi
who died 6th December 1997

The sun of justice shall arise
with healing in his wings.

Malachi 4:2

Light and life to all he brings,
Risen with healing in his wings.

Charles Wesley

Contents

	Prologue	
	Introduction	– 1
1.	A Mother-in Law's Fever	– 11
2.	The Paralysing Power of the Past	– 21
3.	The Astonishing Faith of an Enemy	– 31
4.	Touching the Leper	– 38
5.	Mob Violence	– 47
6.	Wailing for a Sleeping Child	– 56
7.	The Woman at the Edge of things	– 67
8.	The Beggar of Jericho	– 78
9.	The Hidden Healer & the Alien Woman	– 87.
10.	Ephphatha: Open Up	– 94
11.	The Healing Pool	– 102
12.	I Believe: Help my Unbelief	– 110
13.	I was Blind: Now I See'	– 121
14.	Lazarus	– 132
15.	Look, Listen, Live	– 141
16.	The Healing Tree	– 153
	Epilogue : Restoring the Wouned Psyche of a Would-be Guru	– 163

Poems by Jane Sahi

1.	A Hidden Life Unsealed	11-12
2.	The Return	21-22
3.	'I am not worthy to come under your roof'	31
4.	The Touch	38-39
5.	To Bear Such Pain	48
6.	Drawn Back from the Edge	56-57
7.	'Who Touched Me'?	67-68
8.	'Let Me See Again'	78
9.	'He Could Not be Hidden'	87
10.	The Wonder of Sound	94
11.	'Bathe me in the bathing of thy pool'	102-103
12.	'I believe, but ....'	110-111
13.	'Lead me from darkness....'	122
14.	The Further Shore	133-134
15.	The Leap to Life	142

Pictures by Jyoti Sahi

1.	Welcome from Fever	15
2.	Seed Mudra	23
3.	Feathers' Reach	37
4.	Flight	43
5.	Serpent Chained	55
6.	Swan's Cry	63
7.	Heaven's Tide	73
8.	Amazing Love	85
9.	Hidden Healing	90
10.	Listening, Opening	98
11.	In-gathering	107
12.	Wing Tips	120
13.	Wings of Light	129
14.	Life Bearer	139
15.	Winged Dance	151
16.	Lifted up	155

Prologue

When Jesus came in sight of the city, he wept over it and said, 'If only you had known the way that leads to your peace.... How often have I longed to gather your children, as a mother-bird gathers her brood under her wings...' (Luke 19:41-2; 13:34)

Few biblical images are more poignant than this picture of Jesus weeping over Jerusalem - the city on the holy hill, the city that was God's special sign of loving purpose for all people, the sign of healing and peace for all creation; yet a city that was doomed to fall. They were the same tears of compassion that the pain of the sisters of Bethany drew from him when they mourned their brother's death. They are the tears of the heart of the Healer who knows there is no easy way to the healing of all. Words of peace, and the rhetoric of justice, may be easy to speak. But most of us are far from ready to accept the conditions that lead to peace and healing.

So the great heart of God goes on longing, and sharing the pain. The picture Jesus gives us is of an agitated mother-bird, seeking to gather her brood together under her wings. And this is the theme that Jyoti Sahi takes as the central image in the pictures that are his contribution to this book. A single image, but woven into the many different strands of the stories. Jane's poetic imagination too offers many new insights as she draws on a wider range of imagery than do my own more discursive reflections.

By early 1997 the first draft of these reflections were able to be shared with friends at Jyoti's Ashram near Bangalore. On the few occasions he was well enough, Jyoti's father, Shanti, having been very close to death but a few weeks before, was able to be carried out to our meeting place under the trees, and sit with us for a while. On other days he was in great distress, and our meditating on the meaning of healing seemed so much to the point. Unbelievably Shanti gained in strength during the following months; but the end came, with merciful peace, late in the year. We dedicate this book to his memory. It was during the painful days when it was clear Shanti's death was very near that Jyoti quite suddenly was gripped by the image of the divine Healer, manifest as the bird like sun, 'risen with healing in his wings' in the prophetic vision. In Jyoti's pictures, the healing bird is also that frequent figure of Indian devotion and legend, the Hamsa, the fabled heavenly Swan. Though praised for its white purity, the Hamsa is also described as golden like the sun; it is both the bearer and the special offspring of the Creator; it is both wonderfully wise in speech and also noted for its silence; above all is has a loyal, loving, caring heart. And the heavenly Swan is a mysterious healer. Even in European legend the Swan is a figure in which male and female unite, and is one who leads the way across the waters that carry us into the eternal world beyond.

In the Bible too the prominence of bird-imagery is obvious. There are over 300 bird-references. A number of these similarly suggest several different forms of healing, as is clear in Jesus' picture of himself as a brooding mother-bird. We may note here just a few more. 'Look at the birds, said Jesus, 'and like them be free from all those inner anxieties that plague your life' (Matthew 6:25-26). Be free from fear too: 'Trust the loving, caring purpose of your heavenly Father, who notices even the fall of a lowly little sparrow' (10:29). Long before this, Moses had sung of God's liberating action as being like that of an Eagle carrying its young on his wings:

> *May my teaching fall like raindrops,*
> *my words distil like dew,*
> *like lavish showers on growing plants...*
> *God guarded his people as the apple of his eye.*
> *As an eagle watches over its nest, hovers over its young,*
> *spreads its pinions and takes them up,*
> *and bears them on his wings, the Lord alone led his people.*
> *(Deuteronomy 32:2,10-11).*

As is often the case with biblical bird-imagery, though, the song then recalls people's lack of response, and the inevitable loss of freedom, of health, of strength. But Moses not only sings of God's healing; the same caring God sometimes seems to 'inflict wounds'.

This raises the great mystery of human sin and suffering, that was to culminate in the ministry of Jesus the Healer, a mystery that had been struggled with, however inadequately, even from biblical beginnings. It is the Eagle again that provides a key image concerning this mystery. During the time of further loss of freedom and of self-confidence, perhaps the greatest of the prophets again saw the strong flight of the Eagle as a sign of the renewal of life and strength that God's people can yet hope for:

> *God gives vigour to the weary, new strength to the exhausted,*
> *Even the fittest may stumble and fall;*
> *But those who look to the Lord will renew their strength,*
> *They will soar as on eagle's wings....(Isaiah 40 :25 - 31).*

Eagles, sparrows, ravens, swallows, doves, owls, and many more species too, are brought in to illumine the picture of God's ways with the human race. A final image of hope, frequently found, is that of a corporate healing, the healed community - many kinds of birds all gathered for shade and safe roosting in their tree-home, the all-embracing kingdom that is the peaceful reign of God (Ezekiel 17:23; 31:6; Mathew 13:32). For the healing to which the acts of Jesus point is always to be 'corporate' in its fullest sense – seen in the transformation of the ever-widening bodies that make up our being , our world. The Healer of the Gospels, the Sun of Justice, leads us to have faith in, and to struggle for fulness of life for all God's children, for all creation.

Introduction

Surprisingly little has been written on the healing acts of Jesus. And there is almost nothing written on these stories by way of systematic reflection. This is surprising for at least three reasons. There is the fact that healing figures so prominently in the Gospels, especially in Mark. The first half of Mark's story is comprised of almost 50% healing-related material. And what relates to *bodies*, whether of others or that of Jesus himself, accounts for even more of the gospel story.

The gospel-writers, then, clearly want Jesus to be seen as 'The Great Healer'. In fact, Jesus himself takes healing as a paradigm of all he does: 'Only those who are sick need a doctor. I have come to call the outcasts, not those who are respectable.' It would not be too far-fetched even to say that his very name, Jesus—or in the original, Yeshua—could as well mean 'One who heals', as 'One who saves'. For, often in the New Testament, when 'salvation' is used in English for the Greek *soteria*, it is more accurate, as well as carrying a far richer, more concrete meaning, to translate with the New English Bible as 'healing'. 'The grace of God has dawned upon the world with *healing* for all', is the Apostle's description of what was happening because of Jesus (Titus 2:11). So it is perplexing that 'Healing' has not been used more frequently as an interpretive category, as a hermeneutical key, for understanding the faith of those who seek to follow Jesus.

One recent book, Stevan Davies' *Jesus the Healer*, does recognise healing as the central purpose of Jesus' minisrty. But Davies clearly avers that he has no interest in theological meanings, which leads him to ignore substantial parts of the healing acts and sayings associated with them. The stories are subject to Davies' view that Jesus as a spirit-possessed ecstatic, like all shaman-figures, healed by being taken over by another persona; in this state he was able to draw other people into sharing his own 'dissociative religious trance'. This is an unnecessarily limiting interpretation; but there is a potentially important insight running through the book. And such a psycho-anthropological way of reading the stories could prove fruitful especially in trying to wotk out a more authentic Dalit and Tribal theology. Similarly Sudhir Kakar's *Shamans, Mystics and Doctors*, which explores alternative ways of healing (especially mental healing) in an Indian context, could provide some fascinating insights for anyone trying to look at the Gospel stories more comparatively.

It is interesting that the Buddha also took the healing process as paradigmatic of his vision of how humans need to be liberated. In fact, he too was known as 'the Healer'. But it is in the Gospels that stories of healing become so central. There can be no authentic picture of Jesus, no authentic account of his liberating work, unless his healing acts are crucial to that picture. Those early followers saw him as the fulfilment of the prophetic word: 'The sun of justice will arise with healing in his wings' (Malachi 4:2, or 3:20 in the Jerusalem Bible). Certainly we cannot know the meaning of Jesus for our time, for ourselves, for our world, unless it is the *healing Jesus* who is the focus of our reflection. No doubt we need to place this picture of Jesus within the frame of the pain and suffering he himself was subjected to, and the rising from death that is the climax of the story. And this is done in our final chapter, 'The Healing Tree'. Even so, his healing acts, his healing intention, remain crucial.

At least women writers on the Jesus-story are usually more aware of the implications for Christian faith of his healing work, though few have written systematically on it. And this is another reason for surprise that this healing category is so neglected. With the impact of ecological concern in general, and women's emphases in particular, terms like 'healing', 'wholeness', 'the body' occur quite freely now in theological writings. Why, then, this lack of detailed reflection even by feminist writers on the meaning of these healing acts? When particular stories have been interpreted, as by Elisabeth Moltmann-Wendel in *I am My Body*, the result is impressive, even if some exegetical details seem implausible.

A third reason for surprise is the fact that many of these stories are fascinating just *as stories*; they are often very briefly told, but there is great narrative power and drama in them. It takes but little imagination to draw out this dramatic dimension. In general, though, I have refrained from much embellishment of the often quite stark account of how things happened. At a time when Narrative Theology is so popular—the belief that our stories are primary data for faith's reflecting—it is surprising that so little systematic writing is done on these basic faith-stories.

But there are also reasons why we need not be so surprised that more reflective writers keep away from these healing stories. 'Divine healing' has the potential for being a real danger-area. Certain kinds of fundamentalist preachers, with their literalism and special love of the irrational, often have a rampaging field-day with this healing material. These stories, no doubt intended by the Gospel-writers to amaze and evoke a sense of wonder, can so easily be made to fit into a simplistic world-view in which the intrinsic worth of creation, the meaning of the historical process, the positive value of human community relationships and our cultural life, the whole human *context* in which the healing acts occur—all this becomes irrelevant. All that matters is a magic-performing divine power that intervenes entirely from outside that human context. And literalism leaves no room at all for that imaginative hermeneutical task which is surely part of the great command to love God with all our mind, as well as with heart and soul and strength (Luke 10:27).

The Gospels also make it clear that faith in God is of crucial importance if there is to be the healing God intends. In fact, it is even said that Jesus' healing ministry was drastically limited when people did not believe (Mark 6:5). What irrevocable harm is done, though, by those revivalist healers — in India perhaps as much as anywhere — who demand an absolute and unwavering faith in the power of Jesus working through *them* if his acts of healing are to be repeated now. And when an immediate cure does not take place, the sick person is then accused of being too weak in faith, and so is burdened with further guilt. There is the added danger of the 'healer' claiming a crude personal authority, and exploiting the dependence of the sick, in ways that Jesus never did. In fundamentalist hands 'divine healing' can be hugely problematic.

Not that modern medicine has all the answers to our hunger for healing. It too may have its share of 'miracles'; certainly some quite wonderful things have happened in the medical world, from the eradication of such scourges as small-pox, to the growing success of laser and key-hole surgery. Bio-genetics (with all the ethical question it raises) will no doubt perform even greater 'miracles'. Yet, the fact is that growing numbers of people in countries where modern medicine is most advanced are now turning to 'alternative medicine' — herbal remedies, acupuncture, aroma-therapy, yoga, divine healers of many kinds. Modern medical practitioners need the humility to be far more self-critical than has been evident to date. For modern medicine seems, rather than helping us to feel relaxed about health matters, to have made our search for health almost an obsession. Even so, no 'alternative' approach can afford blatantly to ignore all the findings of modern medicine concerning our bodies and minds, as revivalist healers as well as some 'alternative' practioners usually do.

At the other extreme to the fundamentalists, there is a growing tendency among others who also give weight to 'healing' to interpret it in ways that leave out so much that comes through forcefully in these stories of Jesus. I refer to that typical 'New-Age' world-view that speaks *only* in the soothing terms of being 'in tune with one's deeper self', those who see little need for contextual or community engagement, who see no need at all for anger and confrontation as an essential part of the healing process, and who therefore, in an odd way echo the fundamentalist's obsession with the individual, with a privatised view of healing. 'New-Age' approaches are quite right in their desire to return to a life-style more in tune with nature and with earth's hidden powers. In this sense we all need a 'creation-centred' spirituality. Modern medicine has usually missed this truly vital dimension of our human being altogether. But healing also and always has to do both with our relating to *others*, and our recognition that our life has become deeply flawed (in a way that 'creation-centered spirituality' usually overlooks), as well as our relating to the earth-habitat in which God has placed us. There are views of healing, then, that are certainly not in tune with the intention of Jesus, and which weaken the cause of any who rightly want to place healing at the centre of our faith in God, at the centre of our vision of God's world.

Healing, in other words, *can* be a way of focusing more sharply on issues at the centre of *liberationist* concern. These stories of Jesus' healing acts *can* be powerful paradigms of the wholeness we seek for our world, the new world of God's justice we must surely struggle for, whether as front-line activists, or as back-stage supporters with our prayers, our preaching, our thinking. Jesus the Healer is also Jesus the Just, the one whose every act expressed his concern for the promised new world in which all God's children would find acceptance and wholeness, justice and peace. The stories of his healing acts, therefore, are pregnant with wider meaning and point us inexorably to the wider web of life of which we are part. A rapidly growing number of people are now suffering from cancer of the skin caused by the rays of the sun, now made harmful through our damaging of the earth's protective zone layer. This tragic fact could make my title seem rather ironic. The benign 'healing' in the sun's wing-like rays has now turned, through our destruction of earth's life, to harmful and malignant wounding. In our very title, then, we are reminded that healing necessarily has to do with how we relate to earth's life.

Even so, the stories are concerned with particular individuals, for in that economy, or *oiko-nomy*, that is God's way of relating to the human race, indeed to the whole *oikos* that is our eco-habitat, it is in the particular and the personal that God's good purpose becomes known. Each person in each story was of infinite worth to Jesus, as to God. Yet each person also points us to the infinite range of God's concern; their stories point beyond themselves.

In a similar way, my own reflecting on the meaning of these stories for our time arises out of a particular personal history. It is my own 'story' that draws out the particular themes I develop as *the meaning* intended by these healings of Jesus. It can be no other way; for this is God's way. So there is quite frequent reference to the experience of my many years in India, and some reference to my more recent life in inner city Britain. In fact, the Epilogue that I have added is a very personal account of the healing of my own psyche during a painfully difficult time recently. As is mentioned there, the original form of these sixteen reflections on the healing acts of Jesus were meditations given each month in a healing group within which I was both minister and ministered unto. And that very particular context obviously accounts for some of the themes I develop in this book.

The Evangelists write often of the 'amazement' that people felt when they saw the healing work of Jesus. What, as much as anything, amazed me each month — as I faced the task of expounding the meaning of each new story — was the way in which each one was able to bring something new to light, concerning either the loving purpose of God for us, or the nature of our own resistance to that good purpose and our need of God's healing touch.

From time to time people also 'wondered' at the way Jesus was able to point to and make real the 'healing' promised through the prophets. There were very clear instances of this in the prophet Isaiah: 'The blind will be able to see, and the deaf to hear. The lame will leap and dance, and those who cannot speak will shout for joy. Streams of water will flow through the desert . . .'(35:5-6). Or, the promise in Second Isaiah: 'I will heal (my people). I will lead them and help them, and I will comfort those who mourn. I offer peace to all, both near and far. I will heal my people' (57:18-19).

We have already noted how Malachi spoke of that final age of God when 'the sun of justice shall arise, with healing in his wings'. Another speaks of God coming as a true shepherd, 'to look for those who are lost, restore those who have strayed, bandage up those who are hurt, heal those who are sick, leave the healthy and strong to play, and give them their proper food' (Ezekiel 34:16). Another prophet speaks of God's obedient Servant who suffers on behalf of others; it is as though 'he bore our suffering and endured our torments, so that 'the chastising he bore is health for us, and by his scourging we are healed' (Isaiah 53:4-5). The first Gospel specifically relates this prophecy to the self-giving *healing acts* of Jesus, who did not even find time to rest and eat (Matthew 8:17). Many more such passages make it clear that 'healing' here is a key prophetic image picturing the 'salvation', the renewal of earth's life that God promises, when creation's potential and God's good purpose will be realised. This prophetic affirmation of the 'healing' to come surely should be our most clear clue in interpreting the healing stories of Jesus. The prophets, of course, do not give us just one message; diverse streams flow through the 'prophetic tradition'. Even so, there was a single-minded conviction that God was at work in the events of their time, that God will not rest until 'justice is established on the earth', and that true faith in God entails a life in tune with the just ways of God.

So then, there is every reason to think that all that Jesus did and said follows in that prophetic tradition. Indeed, he was known as 'the Prophet of Nazareth'. But one of the identifying marks of a prophet has always been an ability to break out of the constraints of any given cultural tradition, the power to point beyond the conditioning of the present to the possibilities of the future, to God's purposes for our future. And this is what these stories of Jesus are able to do—though only if we allow them to interact dynamically with our life today, in all its perplexity and complexity. Those literalists who try to expound the stories of Jesus only within the cultural framework of his time and place are doomed to miss so much of their meaning and power.

Some, I'm sure, will find my account of who Jesus is, and what he did, inadequate. In general I have reflected within the christological framework that the Gospels themselves (including John's) provide us with. Therefore, his *humanness* is taken as a primary reality. As Christian faith has always affirmed, Jesus is 'fully human'. On the question this still leaves — the question of how Jesus distinctively relates to God — I have made no attempt to speculate, or to draw on the usual formulations. His healing work, with its liberating, transforming potency, its power to evoke wonder, as portrayed in the stories and reflected on in terms of the wholeness we so deeply need, itself points us to categories beyond the ordinary, beyond the 'merely human'.

Indeed, the power of these stories to provoke such reflection, to point to ways in which human life twenty centuries later can be transformed, ways in which the earth can be restored to its wholeness, in itself is testimony to the 'otherness' of Jesus. And from time to time the stories themselves compel us to think of what it means to call Jesus 'the Christ', 'Son of God', 'Light of the World', 'the Resurrection and the Life'. Mostly, though, I have used the simple name 'Jesus' — as in fact the original stories usually do. Coming from the Hebrew 'Yeshua' (or Joshua), as we noted above, the name itself means 'one who saves', and therefore 'one who heals.' Such a name should certainly not be seen as in any way diminishing the distinctive character of this Person who has always been in some way central to Christian faith.

And one last point before we look at the stories themselves. Why is the faith of some Christians seemingly so brittle that they feel threatened by the thought that there are healers other than Jesus in the world? Even in Jesus' own time there were 'wonder-workers' wandering around performing remarkable cures on occasion. And there were sacred shrines and holy pools reputed to be able to heal all manner of sickness. In fact, healing in which some kind of supernatural power is invoked has been important in almost all religions and cultures. Often it is some charismatic, or shamanistic, person who is believed to channel this mysterious power. Devotees of Satya Sai Baba — a 'Bhagavan' from a very lowly rural background in Andhra Pradesh — tell countless stories of instances of healing through his power. Muslims in India turn for healing especially to the burial-places of their saints, as do many others, including Christians in some cultures. Hanuman, the monkey-God, and other animals too, such as the snake, and Hamsa the heavenly Swan, have been revered as having strange healing powers.

The important question, then, is not whether all these healers do or do not have divine power. If they actually heal, then of course they have power, of course they are somehow part of God's healing purpose, just as are all medical people effective in healing those who suffer. The important question rather is: How does such healing, as any healing, fit into the wider purposes of life? What is the contextual meaning of such healing? Within what vision of life does it take place? How does personal healing point us to the wider healing of the body of the human community and the body of God's earth? What does my healing lead on to in life's wider milieu?

In the end there is just one necessary question: What does healing *mean*? And it is this question we shall seek to answer in relation to the many healing acts of Jesus. What do these stories *mean* in relation both to the wider mission of Jesus and to our life today? In what sense are these stories paradigmatic pointers to the healing and wholeness of life we seek for our world, for all creation? The world-view within which we set any acts of healing is all-important.

In the second half of the twentieth century a remarkable faith-movement has been taking place in the eastern delta-areas of India's Andhra Pradesh. Several thousand people, mainly from the fairly prosperous Hindu farming communities there, have been caught up in a surge of new faith in Jesus. They meet in small house-groups, and occasionally in larger gatherings, for song and prayer and Bible-reading. Often there has been little contact with formal church structures (though caste-division partly accounts for this). At least one branch of this movement — that of Subbarao — claims never to have been in touch with any Christian agency. Direct religious vision was their inspiration.

While working in that same area, I asked what was the single most important factor impelling the movement generally. I was told: 'Faith in the healing power of Jesus'. Nearly every person concerned had someone who had been touched by what they believed was his strange healing power, whether through personal prayer or vision, through laying on of hands, or through treatment by a Christian doctor.

And yet, from its beginnings this movement had necessarily to set faith in the strange healing power of Jesus within a wider life-context. There were those who were asked to *interpret* what such healing meant, what sort of life-style it was to lead to, what view of God and of the world it called for, what new purpose for life it compelled. In Kerala, in Tamil Nadu, and probably in other regions too, there are similar centres to which great numbers of people flock with the strong hope of divine healing. 'What does this strange healing mean?', is the question now being asked. And these are precisely the kind of questions Jesus expected his own healing acts to provoke, as well as the parabolic stories he told. For it is just here that we find the crucial difference between one healer and another, indeed between one faith-tradition and another. These too are the questions we shall reflect on as we now look at stories of 'Jesus, the Healer'. What do they mean? In seeking for *meaning*, however, we should not forget that we are dealing here in the first place with *dramatic stories*, stories that describe actions with great symbolic power. What people *saw,* the *scenes* enacted before their eyes were certainly just as important as the accompanying *words* pointing them towards a tentative grasp of their *meaning.* It is in part because these actions are rather like miniature *dramas* that I have divided my account of them into clearly marked sections. In some cases these sections function very definitely as scenes within the drama we are to watch.

This dramatic quality of the stories is also brought out forcefully by the images, created in their different ways by Jyoti and Jane Sahi, in the pictures and poems that accompany the text. The former should not be looked at merely as illustrative pictures quite secondary to the words and ideas I have written. True, they are in tune with the intention of the text. But Jyoti's imagery — with its images of the heavenly Hamsa (Swan) — in its own right enables reflection on the stories, as also does Jane's poetry. I am immensely grateful to them both for their contribution to my own reflection on these healing acts; but whether it is the dramatic imagery or the words and ideas that prove the more helpful to the reader, in the end it is *an inner vision*, attunement with the intention of Jesus, that is what we shall aim for.

Each reflection that follows is preceded by the story as told in the concerned Gospel. The basis for this text is the New Revised Standard Version, as this is the most widely used in India. However, at some points I have diverged slightly from this, where I have felt another translation to be more fitting.

1 A Mother-in-law's Fever

They entered the house of Simon and Andrew, with James and John. Now Simon's mother-in-law was in bed with a fever, and they told him about her at once. He came and took her by the hand and lifted her up. Then the fever left her, and she began to serve them.

That evening, at sundown, they brought to him all who were sick or possessed with demons. And the whole city was gathered at the door. And he cured many who were sick with various diseases, and cast out many demons (Mark 1:29-34).

A Hidden Life Unsealed

She was there
Seen and unseen, but
most noticed
In absence -
Job's weaver's shuttle
Taken for granted
To perform a task
Unasked, unspoken.
She saw little meaning
Herself in the clamour
And movement;
For she barely saw
The fine pattern
Pressed out of her service,
Caught in the threads
And knots of the moment.

But she felt over-used,
Worn down, worn out
And retired to her bed;
It was there that He came
So suddenly beside her.

There was no time for pretence,
No time to make-up
A face for defence;
For he knew
The fire that consumed her.
He took her hand, held
And healed her by
Sharing for a moment
The pulse of a vision
That set alight
The everyday, and once again
Flood lit the drab-grey
Bush of thorns.

The first of our stories is a briefly told but rather touching account of Jesus healing Peter's mother-in-law. Set between two almost frenzied scenes - first the loudly screaming demoniac in the Synagogue, then the hysterical clamour of the crowds 'sick with all kinds of diseases' outside Peter's house and continuing even in 'lonely places outside the town' — here we have a quiet interlude that's a bit of a family affair: there's a sort of tranquil domesticity about this simple story.

Family life, though, is rarely quite as tranquil as it may appear on the outside. Who knows, for example, what kind of mother-in-law jokes may have been bandied around between the little group of Jesus' followers? It's not only western stand-up comedians who tell mother-in-law jokes. The Telugu people, for example, have a saying: 'The bliss in a mother-in-law's house is like a biff on the funny-bone'.

There may be no explicit record of Jesus and the disciples laughing. We're told only of Jesus weeping. Yet, the humour in so many of his sayings makes it impossible that there wasn't laughter also in his presence. And both tears and laughter, in their different ways, can be great healing aids; they can be wonderfully ther apeutic. Just recently a report of research has been published that shows very clearly how potent laughter is for health. It's not that difficult to imagine either Jesus or one of the other disciples having a dig at Peter: 'Hey, Rock-man, you're a big master in the boat, but a little mouse when you're near your mother-in-law!' Perhaps not; but who knows what went on between these earthy fishermen and their ex-carpenter leader whom the strait-laced religionists of his time found far too wild, far too much of a rule-breaking iconoclast, far too much of a fun-lover, a 'glutton and wine-bibber', for their liking. Because of their prudish prejudice they saw nothing of those signs of glory that also broke out in this man's life, in the things he said and did.

Peter, though, had seen them. And finding his mother-in-law ill, told Jesus about her condition. There are three simple features in these two verses that we will reflect on.

I

The *first* is that she was '*sick with a fever*'. Medically, no doubt, it was simply a question of something having caused an infection in the bloodstream, so that she had a raised temperature, and all the symptoms of a feverish condition. The body's defence mechanisms were putting up a strenuous fight against some unwanted invader.

This word 'fever', however, has other connotations, relating to the spirit's inner life. Indian spiritual life often describes that inner turbulence—debilitating, destructive, and above all truth-obscuring states of mind such as anxiety, fear, lust, anger, greed, pride, obsession—as the feverish fires of the spirit. For the Buddha, all these fevered states derive from a basic 'thirst', a deep-rooted 'desire' that is the cause of all the distress, the dis-ease, that always marks our life, like the dis-ease of an ill-fitting wheel on its axle. It is this root-cause, desire, preached the Buddha, that somehow has to be cured, as a physician probes to the root-cause of an illness and prescribes an effective remedy. The 'Noble Eight-fold Way' is offered as just such a cure for this inner fever. The fires of this fever can be snuffed out (the literal meaning of *nirvana*) and eternal peace attained.

The life-style of far too many followers of Jesus, in our times at least, is indeed fevered, and in need of 'cooling and calming'. Our desires are dangerous. But just being human is itself dangerous, and desire is inherent in our humanness. On the one hand it shows our incompleteness, our dissatisfaction with how we now are. And this too is basic to our being as humans. It fuels the process of change, of moving forward in our human journey. So desire also makes us open to the future and to its possibilities for newness. Just as desire can become the cause of fevered disintegration, so also desire can become the cause for openness to the healing purpose of God.

So there was not only the fevered state of that frenzied demoniac in the Synagogue and of the crowds clamouring for cures for their many kinds of diseases. There was also a fever in this home where Jesus had come to enjoy a moment's respite in the company of his small band of newly appointed disciples. But these opening scenes in Mark's Gospel give us a picture of rapidly accelerating agitation throughout Galilee, as a result of what Jesus was doing. Very early the next morning, following the Synagogue healing, we find Jesus slipping out to a lonely place for prayer. The search for him was frantic: first by 'Peter and his companions'. When he is found, Jesus is told: 'Everyone is looking for you'. And this crowd fever is even increased after the leprosy sufferer is miraculously cured. Jesus 'could not go into a town publicly. Instead, he stayed out in lonely places'. But even there, 'people came to him from everywhere.'

There seems to have been very little of that 'Sabbath rest by Galilee, with calm of hills above', where Jesus shared with God the 'silence of eternity', in John Greenleaf Whittier's poetic picture. Even Jesus himself is gripped by a kind of fever: 'I must go on to the other villages around. I have to preach in them also' (Mk 1:38). And at another time an even stronger sense of agitation: 'I came to set the earth on fire; and how I wish it were already kindled. . . Do you suppose that I came to bring peace to the world?' A far cry, it would seem, from the calm serenity, the tranquil indifference, of the ideal Yogi of Indian tradition. His family soon came to believe he'd gone mad, when they found he was not even stopping for proper times of rest and food (Mk 3:21).

But we could easily be misled here. That compelling inner urge to move on, that agitating concern to complete his mission, was grounded in a deep inner confidence in the healing purpose of God.

"WELCOME FROM FEVER"

It is in no way the feverish compulsion just to be doing something, the wild rush for some new experience, the frantic surge to explore new places, to make new products, to possess new goodies - all so typical of our modern consumerist life-style; typical at least of those who have been able to seize control of global resources and feverishly exploit earth's life at the expense of those their life-style cruelly oppresses.

This kind of 'fever' is as much in need of calming and curing as was the sick condition of the crowds who came so frantically seeking him. And the fierce compulsion of Jesus to move on was grounded in his concern that in the rush for a cure, people do not miss the point of it all: that they do not fail to find their life also grounded in the Centre-Point of all being, the Source of all true sharing and healing and well-being. Our frantic search for well-being, for life-enhancement, often itself has disastrous consequences; certainly we are in danger of losing touch with the One who, in the end, is the only Giver of life and healing.

II

And so we move on to the *response of Jesus* to this woman's condition. For 'as soon as he arrived, he was told about her.' His response was immediate: 'He went to her, took her by the hand, and helped her up.'

These three actions are so typical of the healing work of Jesus. 'He went to her', focusing on this particular person, a person seen as quite distinct from anyone else, unique in the midst of so much frantic need all around. Countless people have, through this Jesus, found faith in a God with whom they are able to relate, a God who 'comes' to them directly, who sees them in their utter uniqueness, even as he does the millions of others in their need too. This multi-relational knowledge and presence and power is what it means to be 'God', they have found. And none of our quite proper talk of 'Source' and 'Centre-point' should blur this intensely *personal face of God*.

In Jyoti's picture 'Welcome From Fever', the wings of the heavenly Swan, the Hamsa, are stretched envelopingly around the sick woman, like fans to cool her fever. The wings touch her as though they are hands encouraging and lifting her up, while her hands are stretched out imploringly. For the wing-feathers of a bird do function in some ways like hands. As well as being used to protect nestlings from heat, cold and rain, various signals are given through the wings - to attract a mate, to threaten an enemy, to entice a prey. Wings communicate, are used to 'touch'. And, as we shall see in the sixteen pictures of Jyoti's, in Indian tradition, the heavenly Swan 'touches' humans in many different ways, not least as a healer. In this story the Hamsa, Jesus, is both received into the home as a guest, and is also one who welcomes the sick woman to himself for healing. For the Swan is often depicted as a welcoming figure carved on the doors of houses. So the healing, welcoming hands of Jesus restore this woman within her home.

Then it is said that Jesus 'took her by the hand'. Again and again the hands of Jesus feature prominently in his healing acts. It is through our hands that we express so much. The eyes too may be powerfully expressive of what is in us. But it is our hands that are the more tangible, palpable extension of our bodies. I was made very aware of the fact recently when my friend Brother Arul, one of the Little Brothers who do an outstanding ministry of healing and helping in their unobtrusive way, showed me a fascinating collection of pictures of the hands of people in a hundred different situations, many of these culled from the French magazine of mission, *Prier*.

Healing power, even if but faintly, probably flows through the hands of many more of us than we realise; not just through the few known as 'healers', who in some cases become quite charlatanic in their exploiting the credulity of people in need. But the hands of some do, very clearly, transmit an 'odic force' that, in varying degrees, hastens the healing process. In the Epilogue to this book, I write of the effect of such healing hands on my own distressed condition not long ago: healing hands of a group of otherwise quite ordinary people.

It is sad, perhaps tragic, that it is almost taboo in some cultures to touch one another, especially those of the other sex. In some of the tribal communities of India, unless there has been the touch and holding of hands — by men, women and children — it is felt that there has been no real meeting. Some conservative traditions in India are very different, of course, though holding of hands between men and men, and women and women, is far more common here than in western countries. And there, anti-gay feeling, feminist resentment of male sexual harassment, and growing anxieties about paedophilia and the sexual abuse of children, have now made quite innocent touching of men or women or children a very explosive issue. As feminists very rightly insist, of course any unwanted touching is out.

And yet, whatever the dangers of abuse in a more free approach to the human touch, forbidding it — even to doctors in some cultures — imposes great restraints on the potential we have to be healers to each other. For a few, anyone's touch is threatening. But there are many, many more who witness to the 'blessing' received, perhaps when they were ill and fearful in hospital, and a minister, or counsellor, or nurse, or friend held their hand. It was not just 'comforting'; it may well have helped the healing.

Certainly for Jesus, it was through his hands that healing so often flowed out to others. In this case Jesus 'took her hand', and this was specifically in order *'to help her up', to lift her to her feet.* This image of lifting people up to 'stand on their own feet' powerfully expresses what has to happen in true healing. For healing is very much a matter of providing a person with the resources for the healing process to take place within them. The good doctor or surgeon — those with sufficient humility - will confess they in reality heal no one. They merely provide the right conditions, adequate resources, by which the concerned organism can recover itself. Healing happens when the body can stand on its own feet. Healers are those who provide the resources by which this takes place.

And whatever divine power Jesus brought into this world of need, or into the needy world of those he met, on many occasions we find him enabling people to discover their own resources. No doubt the most outstanding case was when a distraught father pleaded for his wildly epileptic son to be healed: 'Have pity on us and help us, if you possibly can.' 'Yes', said Jesus, 'if you yourself can! Everything is possible for the person who has faith.' But we look at this story more closely in 'I Believe: Help my Unbelief'.

III

Finally, helped to her feet, recovered from her fever, '*she began to serve them*'. In this case of Peter's mother-in-law, no doubt, being healed meant she was able to take up again her life of caring for the house, preparing and serving food, being useful to everyone—her children, grandchildren, guests. And for many people, women and men, becoming ill or incapacitated in some way, grieves them mainly because they can no longer be 'useful'.

Any counsellor, any pastor, will have so often had to assure people, that their worth cannot be measured by the amount of work they do. They *are* persons of value in themselves, apart from their use through what they do. Our *being* is prior to and of greater importance than our *doing*. We can go further than this, of course, and assure people who are perhaps chronically ill that even their helplessness, their need of nursing from others, is of 'value' to others. It is precisely because people are in need of our help, that the serving professions — doctors, nurses, counsellors, ministers, pastors — are able to find in their work the satisfaction that they do. 'You are helping us', is one reply, however inadequate, that I often gave to people despondent because they feel their illness gives trouble to others.

And then, there are people whose suffering has somehow become a means of their being better able to help others. Obviously, when an illness is terminal, or is chronically debilitating, it is bordering on blasphemy to suggest to such a sufferer that their experience will somehow make them better people, that it will act as a refining fire for their inner being. However much suffering is an intrinsic part of our created being, however true that it *can* become redemptive — as Jesus leads us to see — suffering should never be thought of as in itself a good thing for our souls, which some forms of spirituality have done in the past. Suffering for the sake of some good and great cause — now that *can* be ennobling.

Quite apart from that, however, we often find that people who have gone through certain kinds of suffering are certain it has helped them to be better able to help others. The number of women who suffer, and often die, from breast cancer in western countries is now phenomenally high. But it is those who have been through it, and are recovering, who are usually of greater help to those now suffering from it. It's not always the case, of course, if only because some conditions are far less dangerous than others. But I have no doubt that going through a period of severe Depression myself has made me far more sensitive to the needs of others who may be experiencing the pain and disorientation of an illness many still dismiss as merely giving way to self-pity: the pull-yourself-together brigade. The disease itself gives a whole new awareness of what is involved, in a way that merely reading about it can never do.

The Apostle Paul writes of being able to 'comfort others because we ourselves went through suffering and were comforted' (2 Cors 1). And the basis of that 'comfort', or 'strengthening', is the new hope, the new strength, the new possibilities for our future, that *God* has given us — especially in lifting up Jesus from the hopelessness of death. And every time that Jesus took someone by the hand and lifted them up, perhaps when they seemed like dead (as they said of the daughter of Jairus, and of the epileptic son), Jesus was in a way pointing us forward to what was to happen in his own being, his own body.

Healing is never just a private and personal blessing. The healing of a person is always part of the healing and helping of some larger body. For we belong to each other. In one form or another, often hidden from us, we feel each other's pain too. This inter-wovenness of life is part of our embodiedness. So the healing of one body has consequences for other parts of the larger body — the fabric of our social body, our body politic, even the body of creation.

At this point I must acknowledge how deeply indebted I am to the Indian vision (especially in various forms of *bhakti*-faith) that sees the whole universe as the *body* of God. Once we take the body as epiphanic of divine reality in this way, then naturally all embodiedness takes on a sacral quality; we become ever more aware of the mystery and value of our own as well as of other bodies — including those wider expressions of embodiedness in the social body and earth's body. We begin, though, right where we are, with those body-friendly acts that *we* are able to do, perhaps that we *alone* are able to do. For Peter's mother-in-law this meant helping to serve the guests who had come to the house. They included Jesus; but they always do, according to what Jesus himself tells us. It is an act of great blessing, as though done to Jesus himself, he says, to 'give even a cup of water to one of these the least of my brothers or sisters'.

However grand may be, must be, our vision of a new community with fair shares for all, our vision of a new creation with all the earth treated as though it were the beloved body of God, Jesus stresses again and again that we are first to be faithful in small acts of mercy, relating to the body of our world at those points where we first touch it. This is the way we shall show that we have indeed been healed; that our fever has been calmed; that we have been taken by the hand of a Healer whose body is for the making of peace for the whole of the earth; that we have been lifted up to serve — according to that special vocation God has for each of us — to serve his world-wide body in its great need.

2 The Paralysing Power of the Past

When he returned to Capernaum after some days, it was reported that he was at home. So many gathered around that there was no longer room left for them, not even in front of the door; and he was speaking the Word to them. Then some people came, bringing to him a paralyzed man, carried by four of them. And when they could not bring him to Jesus because of the crowd, they removed the roof above him; and after having dug through it, they let down the mat on which the paralytic lay. When Jesus saw their faith, he said to the paralytic, 'Son, your sins are forgiven.' Now some of the scribes were sitting there, questioning in their hearts, 'Why does this fellow speak in this way? It is blasphemy! Who can forgive sins but God alone?' At once Jesus perceived in his spirit that they were discussing these questions among themselves; and he said to them, 'Why do you raise such questions in your hearts? Which is easier, to say to the paralytic, "Your sins are forgiven," or to say, "Stand up and take your mat and walk"? But so that you may know that the Son of Man has authority on earth to forgive sins— he said to the paralytic—'I say to you, stand up, take your mat and go to your home.' And he stood up, and immediately took the mat and went out before all of them; so that they were all amazed and glorified God, saying, 'We have never seen anything like this!' (Mark 2:1-12)

The Return

In the journey down
He felt stripped bare,
Foolish before the crowd,
Exposed to each one's stare —
A comic strip
Of sinking despair;
He saw the pity in
Their glance, but just below
The grinning of derision.

It was a journey inward
Meeting face to face
The slipping skins
That had plaster-cast
His limbs, his life.

The journey home
Seemed not so far
Now that he walked,
His head, his step, his mat
Light-high.
And he returned where he began,
A forgiving and forgiven man.

There is no healing story with quite the dramatic flair of this paralytic who came through the roof. The setting — as with several others — is the frenetic clamour caused among the local populace as a result of outstanding acts of healing by Jesus. To cure one suffering from leprosy, for example, was believed to be as good as bringing back a person from the dead. And that's what this 'Prophet of Nazareth' was said to be doing.

Capernaum, rather than Nazareth, seems to have been the centre for this early Jesus-movement. And when people heard that 'he was at home', they came flocking around, crowding every corner of the house, the courtyard and outside the door. 'There was no room left'; an echo of the way things were at Bethlehem too when Mary gave birth to Jesus. But there it had been the census crowds that had pushed the pregnant Mary, carrying Jesus, outside to the cattle shed; here it was the crowd frantically eager to see what Jesus would do and hear what he had to say that kept the four men, carrying their paralysed friend, outside in the street.

I

The *first* feature of the story that stands out is the *persistence* and the *ingenuity* of these four friends. Or they may have been relatives. Finding there was apparently no way to reach Jesus, they were not prepared to leave it at that. They were not willing just to

"SEED MUDRA"

wait around in the hope that the crowds might drift off later in the day; or return home with the vague thought that another day might be more convenient. They had come to place their friend before the Healer, and they remained determined that this should happen that same day.

So they carried the paralysed man up the side stairs on to the roof. From there they somehow opened up a sufficient gap, then lowered their friend down to Jesus. What a dramatic moment! The kind of drama the crowd would have loved. And it was exactly the kind of single-minded determination that *Jesus* loved to see; he so often praised it in one form or another. Here he calls it an act of great 'faith'. And it was because of that faith — imaginative irrepressible, daring, obstinate faith — that Jesus so readily accepted the challenge to heal this man.

Three smaller matters arise from this opening scene. As we shall see, other stories also bring out the immense value of the help, the encouragement, the prayers of *others* in the healing process; a support group in one form or another is needed by everyone, not only those with exhausting roles as carers and counsellors and ministers. If the family, or informal friendships, provide such support, all the better.

There is also the specific need for help in *locating* Jesus, in *identifying* where the Healer is to be found, how he is to be approached —when so much in life serves to crowd this Source of blessing out from our life-experience. We may well find from time to time we have a mental block, a sort of paralysis of the spirit that makes us feel distanced, quite alienated from any divine Source of inner healing. We all, at times, need the guidance, the carrying, of others to re-locate that Source.

And thirdly, there is the act of *lowering down* the paralysed friend into the place of healing.

In Jyoti's 'Seed Mudra' the paralytic is being lowered from above in a seed-like hammock. The wings are stretched up like the mudra *of a dancer, a gesture of flight, which is what dance often aspires to. Received from below by the wings of the Heal-*

ing Bird, he is embraced, gathered in, and given new life, a new beginning.

Is there a sense in which there can be no healing without some kind of 'going down'? In Aurobindo's elaborate system of 'Integral Yoga', *descent* is essential prior to any hoped-for elevating of the inner self to a higher state. He makes the same point in his long poem, *Savitri*. Savitri has to descend into the underworld if she was to effect her husband's healing. This all reflects the emphasis in Indian *bhakti* stories on the 'going-down' — both the self-effacing 'going down' of the seeker in the presence of divine blessings and the 'going down', the *avatara*, of God into a needy world.

Such a pattern is especially clear in the saving way of Jesus. In several cases of healing there is this descent - down into the water, for example, as in the 'Healing Pool' story; or falling to the ground, down to earth, prior to the lifting up to wholeness, as in the story I've entitled 'I Believe: Help my Unbelief'. Even more striking is the 'descent' of Jesus himself: 'He came down to earth from heaven', as the popular Christmas carol puts it; he 'went down' into Jordan's waters in his baptism; he was lowered down from the cross, laid low in a tomb in the earth; 'He descended into the world of the dead', in the formulation of one the earliest creeds. A whole series of descents are pictured, leading finally to the rising up in resurrected life, spoken of as the 'first-fruits of the new creation'.

Does our own restoration to wholeness, therefore, not also call for this same 'descending', being lowered down, before there is healing and restoration to new life?

II

The *second* dramatic item in this story is the *unexpected* word Jesus spoke to the paralysed man: 'My son, your *sins are forgiven*.' At first, seemingly, no mention of healing! And did not Jesus say elsewhere very clearly that a person's suffering is not caused directly by that person's sin, or by the sin of the parents of that person, which is no doubt what the religious teachers who were watching all this liked to believe? But what they did not like to hear was some travelling preacher/healer like Jesus claiming to forgive people's sins.

So why did Jesus speak of 'forgiveness' in this context? Was this man's problem a matter of the body, or of the soul? Was it caused by a physical disease, or was it of spiritual or psychological origin - was it psycho-somatic? In his response to this man's need, Jesus makes a strong link between the man's *inner* condition and the *outer* symptom. A clear connection is made between some deep-seated wound to his psyche, and the weakness of his body; between something in his past — a trauma to his psyche, his soul — and his state of paralysis.

In both ancient and modern medical practice there have been countless such cases where inner trauma has led to outer inertia; where perhaps a sense of guilt, even if guilt for no consciously identifiable misdeeds, has led to inability to act, or to irrational action and irrational feelings about any action taken - in other words, to a state where part of one's being is immobilised, paralysed. Anyone who has suffered from Clinical Depression will know only too well this state of being unable to function normally; it is not just a matter of feeling somewhat down in spirit. There is a paralysis of normal functioning. Some trauma of the spirit has effectively immobilised activity — even if feelings, imagination, the sense of anxiety and panic, even a sense of self-loathing, may be working in frantic over-drive. 'Your sins are forgiven', was the first approach Jesus made in reaching this paralysed man. Setting him free from a sense of guilt was the first step in setting him free from his bodily malfunction. In effect Jesus is saying: 'Something in your past has broken down the connectedness of your body-soul being. Your wholeness has disintegrated, and you need to be set free and restored within, as part of being restored in body.' The story gives no hint as to what it was lay at the root of this paralytic's trauma. Modern psycho-therapy would certainly want to dig back into the man's childhood or youth. There is no point here in trying to speculate. What is clear in this man's case is that *he believed he was free from this burden from his past, because of the word of forgiveness from Jesus.*

To be 'forgiven', would of course mean in this context more than simply feeling 'I'm OK, you're OK', after the manner of one typical recent form of psycho-therapy. The God-factor is at the centre of this story of forgiveness; on this point the Jewish Teachers were right. But we shall look at 'forgiveness' a little more fully in a moment.

In what ways, then, are we immobilised by our past? When we speak of the 'burden of the past', we are bound to think of the Indian belief in the power of *karma*. This idea that our actions in the past, in previous embodiments we have passed through, determine what we are now was once all-pervasive in Indian religious assumptions. All the great systems in ancient India — Jainism, Buddhism, Hinduism in its many forms — took this belief for granted. The freedom, the *mukti*, or *moksha*, we are all in need of is freedom from this binding chain from our past. It is, of course, the *bad* actions from our past that have 'marked' us with those character-flaws that so hinder the development of our true being. Only some radical way of breakthrough can help us escape from this burden from the past. And this is exactly what the various 'ways' offered by the great Gurus — Jaina, Buddhist, Hindu — claim to achieve: freedom for a new future.

This is not the place to explore the relative merits of these 'ways'. We shall merely note the power of this belief in the binding effect of the past. How many times I have heard ordinary village people exclaim in anguish when some tragedy has struck; 'This is my karma; what great sin have I done?' Modernity has eroded such belief considerably; for it has often taken the form of a fatalism that prevents change, that bars any forward movement.

And yet, we *are* in fact 'bound' by our past. There is so much about each of us as individuals, certainly so much about our social and national, and increasingly even our global, life - assumptions, attitudes, prejudices, feelings, ways of speaking to others, ways of acting in relation to others, ways of structuring our economies -so much that in our best moments we *know* to be undesirable, yet seem helpless to change. We are paralysed, oppressed by our past. Even when we are able to muster enough energy to take revolutionary action, it seems merely to lead to further forms of oppressive bondage.

Not that *all* that comes to us from the past, that makes us what we are, is to be thought of as oppressive. If that were so, there would be no hope at all. The past, our traditions, the cultures our forbears have passed on to us, *can* often be inspiring, supportive, liberating. It is the task of re-shaping, of re-forming our heritage (the *aggiornamento* that good Pope John spoke of), so that it is supportive and liberating for the wider human community, so that there is the freedom to open ourselves to others who are not like us, it is this task about which we find we become paralysed, unable to move effectively.

III

And so to the *third* dramatic moment in the story: the *indignant response* of the religious leaders of the time. They too — the ultra-religious Pharisees and experts in religious Law — were 'paralysed' by their past. It was when Jesus began to talk of forgiveness that they became so indignant: 'How dare he talk like this! This is blasphemy! Only God can forgive sins!' And they were right to insist that it is God alone who forgives sins. The question is, though, *in what ways* does God forgive the tragic consequences of human misdoings? In what ways does God set us free from the bondage of our past wrongs? And set us free from the wrongs done to us? Both are equally important.

The story of a feast follows next in Mark's Gospel. And this is no accident. It was a feast that, again, the puritan Pharisees found offensive. For Jesus was feasting with those that the 'truly' religious people kept away from: outcasts from good society, and those regarded as national traitors because they collected taxes for the occupying enemy. They had invited him to this feast because he had invited them to join his followers. They were all boisterously glad together because God was opening up a miraculous new chance in life.

Of course they were 'wrong' to be taxing their own people on behalf of an occupying force. Of course they were 'wrong' to be prostitutes. Of course the fishermen among them used the 'wrong' language and had the 'wrong' manners for those who would be God's people. But all of them had also *been wronged*: wounding, insulting words had been spoken against them, wounding, insulting actions done against them. In all kinds of ways they were people who needed the break-through of God's forgiveness, needed the sense that they could begin again. But they were also people who knew they were 'sick', knew they 'needed a doctor', to use the words of Jesus in reply to the Pharisees' criticism: 'Why does he eat with such people?' They were all glad together because, through the 'daring' talk of Jesus, they had come to believe they could begin again. This is what forgiveness means.

But there is another aspect of forgiveness, implicit in the glad feasting of the outcasts so looked down on by 'those who have no need of the physician', and perhaps even more necessary to the healing process. There can be no healing — either within ourselves or in our relations with other — unless we also learn how to forgive those who have done harm to us. Jesus spoke of this need again and again, even asserting that there is no forgiveness for us unless we ourselves have learnt to be forgiving of others (Matthew 6:14-15).

The problem is, our natural instinct is to nurture hurt deep within. Resentment and the need for revenge and satisfied honour may not be formal vendetta systems in our way of life, but few of us find it easy to forgive. Forgiveness is refusing to allow the wrong done by another to scar our memory, refusing to allow a wounding word or act to stand between ourselves and those who inflicted the wound. Without forgiveness the result is not just soured or stunted relations, perhaps even retaliation by way of violent words and violent actions. Resentment, like all nurtured hatreds, is like a cancerous growth within our selfhood, taking over, maligning, disfiguring, destroying other cells of our inner being. There can be no wholeness within, nor in our relations with others, unless we learn how to forgive as well as how to accept forgiveness.

To return to the crowded house and the paralysed man. What Jesus firmly asserts in this story is that the 'Son of Man has authority on earth to forgive sins.' We will not here explore the meaning of this special title Jesus uses of himself. It's enough to say that it brings out both his sense of identity with the *human family*, and the hope of God's people that God's outstanding Man would come to restore what was wrong.

What is so unexpected in what follows is how Jesus equates such forgiveness, the putting aside of what is wrong, setting free from the consequences of past wrongs, with setting this man free from his paralysis. In effect Jesus says: 'If I have the power, the right, to heal this man's body, I also surely have the power, the right, to heal his soul. For these are not two separate things. They are two sides of the same coin; both are signs of how God is at work making people's lives whole, opening up a new future for anyone who is willing to open themselves to this new way. Is it easier, in your eyes, to say "You are forgiven", or to say, "Rise up and walk"? As a clear sign of my authority to speak of what God is doing among us, I now say exactly this: "Rise up and walk".'

And to their amazement that is just what happened. Jesus *did* have authority to set people free from a past that paralysed them. Sadly, those who felt they had a monopoly on divine authority still could not accept what he was saying and doing. Their minds were closed to such new possibilities. They were locked into their past. They believed that divine forgiveness was dependent upon the formal procedures that their tradition had set up — the properly confined exegesis of the divine Word, the Law, and the properly ritualised channels of atonement. God had said and done quite sufficient in the past for the faithful to live by. Anything that went beyond this was 'blasphemy'. Jesus was a blasphemer.

Actually Jesus went even further than claiming just for *himself*, as 'Son of Man', the power to forgive sins and heal the inner being. He later made it clear that all those who shared in his way, those who were 'sent out' to heal and bless as he had been sent, they also shared his 'authority to forgive sins', and to set people free from whatever it was that bound them to their past, whatever was traumatising their present, paralysing their whole being (Matth 16:19; 18:18; John 20:23). And no one should be surprised at this. For this setting free from the past is at the centre of the way of Jesus, as it is of the heart of God.

IV

The *final* dramatic moment is when the paralysed man, in response to the authoritative word of Jesus, 'stood up, picked up his mat, and without hesitation went home'. The 'amazement' of everyone there was because of the immediate physical cure, and the power of the word of Jesus that had effected this cure. In spite of the talk of forgiveness, probably many missed the deeper level of healing. Is this not why, very soon after according to Mark, Jesus began to speak 'in parables', and increasingly spoke of the need for secrecy regarding his acts of healing? People were missing the point, the inner meaning of what was happening. They were obsessed with the outer drama.

The ability of people like this paralytic, in response to the word or touch of Jesus, to 'stand on their own feet' and move by their own volition, is a key moment in many of the healing stories. They are no longer in the grip of whatever force, whatever trauma from the past, held them. The point is made even more clearly here by his picking up his mat and walking off home. His mat was the most potent possible sign of his paralysis, his immobility, his bondage. That which previously had carried him, he now picked up and carried off home. 'Home', too, was the place where previously he'd been confined, the place where no doubt he'd spent many hours brooding, perhaps inwardly raging at his impotent state, utterly dependent on the actions of others for his existence. And now he was free. Free to be at ease in his own home, free to be at ease in God's world — that wider human 'home', free to be at ease with himself, free to be at ease with God. All this because, as the story began, 'Jesus was at home'.

3 The Astonishing Faith of an Enemy

Jesus... entered Capernaum. A centurion there had a slave who was very dear to him, and who was ill and close to death. When he heard about Jesus, he sent some Jewish elders to him, asking him to come and heal his slave. When they came to Jesus, they appealed to him earnestly, saying, 'He is worthy of having you do this for him, for he loves our people, and it is he who built our synagogue for us.' And Jesus went with them, but when he was not far from the house, the centurion sent friends to say to him, 'Lord, do not trouble yourself, for I am not worthy to have you come under my roof; therefore I do not presume to come to you. But only speak the word, and let my servant be healed. For I also am a man set under authority, with soldiers under me; and I say to one, "Go," and he goes, and to another, "Come," and he comes, and to my slave, "Do this," and the slave does it.' When Jesus heard this, he was amazed at him, and turning to the crowd that followed him, he said, 'I tell you, not even in Israel have I found such faith.' When those who had been sent returned to the house, they found the slave in good health (Luke 7:1-10; but also see Matthew 8:5-13).

'I am not worthy to come under your roof.'

A door was opened
The Word brimmed in.
Inside out
Or outside in,
Jew or Gentile
Roof or sky
Slave or owner
Under, over
Outcast drawn in
Drawn out
To hear, see, taste
The feast within.

He was an officer of an occupying army, the sworn enemy of true Israelites. Yet he is the hero of our healing story today, for which we need to refer to two Gospels to get a complete picture. At least four qualities stand out in this enemy officer that are the cause of both surprise and praise on Jesus' part.

I

In the *first* place, he was clearly a man of unusual *humanity*, even *compassion*. His servant was said to be 'very dear' to him. And when this servant became very ill, his concern and alarm was such that he sent friends to plead for the healing help of Jesus. (Matthew's Gospel records that he came in person).

The master-servant and master-slave relationship was deeply embedded in the social life of the time; as, indeed, it still is in many societies today. In India, for example, many of the large and growing 'middle-classes' feel very hard done by when they are no longer able to speak of 'my servant', or preferably 'my servants'. Some of us prefer to speak of our 'house-help'; the reality is we are still part of the same system: those who have the power to employ, and those who are employed, and therefore only have such power as together they create for themselves. Among domestics, bonding together in unions is very rare. In the big cities change is afoot. But domestics have usually been so completely dependent on and exploited by their employers, that there is little room left for human dignity: their wages (with food and other perks) are so low it beggars belief; they may be expected to work, with almost no holidays, up to 18 hours a day, seven days a week; and they are sometimes treated with little more respect than scavenging dogs. Obviously there are many exceptions; but one can imagine that the situation often could have been very similar in the world of Jesus' time. It certainly was in the Victorian England of Dickens' time.

And yet, whatever may be our vision of new and more just structures for our society, it is possible for human dignity, the gentle respect due to a fellow-member of God's human family, to be nurtured and to flourish even within a world where there is still colossal injustice. It *is possible* for love and compassion to blossom, for mutual respect to flower, even while our human society is far from fair in its structures.

And such seems to have been the case with this Roman officer, very much the master in his household, in his relations with his servant. He loved him dearly. Quite possibly he was not only loved, but was given great responsibilities, and therefore no little status, within the house. He was loved *and* respected. Our enemy officer was a person with a lot of humanity. And the Gospel story clearly approves.

II

Secondly, this Roman officer *shared in the faith-life of others*. He was willing to use his position of authority and his control of funds even to have a Synagogue built for the local congregation of the Jewish religion. What this man shows, then, is far more than mere tolerance of others' faith, however quaint or strange it may seem. When the Elders from that congregation came to Jesus on his behalf, they were effusive in their praise of this foreigner's friendly and helpful spirit. He is even said to 'love our people'; an alien who refused to allow their great cultural differences to alienate them; an 'enemy' officer, of an occupying power, who refused to accept estrangement.

These Elders assume that Jesus too will be impressed by this Roman officer's interfaith attitude. And he was. In fact, there is almost no evidence in Jesus' words and acts, in the Spirit of Jesus, of the intolerant zeal we find in many of those, today as in previous times, claiming to be true believers. When his followers became incensed at the magical use of the name of Jesus by a wonder-worker who did not belong to their group, Jesus says: 'Those who are not against us, must be for us.' And when soon after the disciples want to bring down fire from heaven on a non-Jewish Samaritan village that was unwilling to welcome Jesus, he found their reaction quite wrong (Lk 9:49-55). When he wanted to illustrate what it means to be a true neighbour, a loving neighbour, he chooses one of those alien Samaritans, a man who was seen by fellow-Jews as far from the true God, and by Jesus' disciples as far from true faith. And in this

Roman officer Jesus finds greater faith than in any of the 'true' people of God.

True, Jesus had very harsh things to say about people, especially religious people, who prove to be stumbling-blocks to the new things God is doing in the world; or who mislead the 'little ones', those who are powerless and vulnerable to others' evil influence. Where there is evil, where people are unjustly oppressed, there must be the courage to speak out. But to identify such evil with those who are not Christian, or do not consciously name Jesus as Lord and Saviour, is to be dangerously out of tune with the Spirit of Jesus. None of those texts which speak of the 'one Name', or the 'true Way', when examined carefully, lead us to think of other names as being demonic, or of other ways as being completely false.

No doubt this issue of how faith in Christ relates to other kinds of faith is immensely complex, and cannot be resolved by superficial slogans. It needs to be struggled with long and strenuously. But above all in this arduous journey of faith, we need to welcome as fellow-pilgrims those from other faiths who, like this Roman officer, share our humanity, our concern for the healing of our world, perhaps even are impressed by the power of Jesus to heal our life.

III

In the *third* place we are struck, as Jesus would have been too, by the *genuine humility* of this Roman officer. Few today give much value to this quality. Self-assertion is seen as the key to personal well-being. Humility tends to be equated with servility and the kind of false obsequiousness of a Dickens' character. Any self-effacing person must surely be hiding the dangerous anger and aggression that lurks beneath.

This Roman's humility is of a very different kind. It is really an expression of the *humanity* of the man's heart. He seems to give little weight to the power-status that was his simply because he was an officer in the greatest military power on earth, and that he represented that power in an occupied land — indeed, a land of military and political nonentities, even if spasmodic trouble-makers, as far as Rome was concerned. This officer defied the opinion of his peers, and accepted the Jewish people as equals. All the in-built arrogance of the power he represented, all their strong sense of racial and national superiority, nurtured so intensely in the military circles of which he was part — all such feelings were thrown off by this man, as he accepted the Jewish people as his *friends*.

It is equivalent to a quite high-ranking officer of the British army in India in the old days of the Raj — if India were about one hundredth of its actual size and global importance — shaking off his fellow officers' absolute assurance of Indian inferiority, and becoming their close friends, even building a Temple, or a Gurdwara for them. Accepting them as social and cultural equals. It is this kind of humility, clearly, that is also the only basis for the kind of interfaith friendship described above. As a matter of historical fact, there were just a few British who were able to become genuine friends of Indians and of Indian culture. But they were few indeed. The pressures against it were immense.

This Roman's sense of being an equal with the Jewish people the army had planted him among takes a different form in his approach to Jesus. Jesus is seen as one of their holy teachers, a great man of God, and he feels he has no right even to be in the presence of Jesus, or to ask him to enter his home. He should keep his distance from such a holy person. On one occasion we find even the impetuous and far from diffident Peter voicing the same feelings, when he saw the great catch of fish following the word of Jesus to 'push out into deep water': 'Leave me, Lord, for I am a sinful man.' And the Gospels tell us that it was quite common for evil spirits to cry out in this way: 'Leave us alone, for you are the Holy One.' It's interesting that the last witness to Jesus at the end of his life was that of a Roman officer who was awe-struck by the signs accompanying his death: 'Truly this was a son of God', that is, an unusually holy person. He was not the first Roman officer to feel this way about Jesus.

And without real humility, there can be no sense of the holiness in the lives of others, or in traditions other than our own; there can certainly be no growth of holiness in our own lives. These words of the alien officer are used in our eucharistic tradition to epitomise the mind we should have when approaching the holy table of the

Lord. Martin Luther — a man in whom, along with his great qualities, there were so many tensions, obstacles to holiness of which he was well aware — took these same words and developed them into a full-blown 'prayer of humble access': 'Lord, I am not worthy that you should enter. . . .'

IV

Finally, there is the strength of this man's *faith* that Jesus praises. In fact, Jesus was quite astonished by it. It was a faith that accepted that there is absolute healing authority merely in the *word* of Jesus. Nothing else was necessary for his servant to be healed. 'Just say the word, and it will be done.' Then he refers to his own experience of command-structures within a military regime in which the discipline of the oath, the 'sacramentum', every soldier made, was absolute. 'I only have to give the command, and it will be done. That's how it is with you too.' No wonder Jesus was astonished. No wonder he holds this up as the strongest faith he had seen anywhere in Israel.

And that faith, the faith of an alien, enemy Roman, becomes for Jesus a pointer to the wider healing that is promised for our world. The healing of sick, needy persons may be a work of great moment in itself. But it leads us forward to a faith in God's healing of the whole human family. So Jesus 'assures' those following him: 'Many will come from the east and the west and will sit down to share in the great feast of God's kingdom' (Matth 8:11).

Here is promised the healing of the wounds that have so painfully over the years torn apart the body of humanity. Vicious racism, cruel ethnic cleansing, the destruction of others' cultures, the demeaning of others' gender, the impoverishing of the powerless — the picture of our global history makes painful reading. But we are promised that healing is possible, that togetherness is God's purpose for us. And we are also warned: if we do not accept this way of healing, of a new togetherness, if we persist in opposing the healing ways of God, in the end there is only the 'outer darkness', with the remorse and pain of final estrangement from God that this entails.

"FEATHERS' REACH"

In Jyoti's 'Feathers' Reach' the wings of the bird take on a new aspect: they are shown as powerfully penetrating, as though breaking through defences. They are still the healing rays of the sun, penetrating even to the recumbent servant within the fortress-like house of the Roman military officer. As with all liberating rays of light, though, they also challenge and turn things upside down - the main point of Jane Sahi's poem earlier.

4 Touching the Leper

A leper came to him begging him, and kneeling he said to him, 'If only you are willing, you can make me clean.' Moved with anger, Jesus stretched out his hand and touched him, and said to him, 'I am willing. Be made clean!' Immediately the leprosy left him, and he was made clean. After sternly warning him he sent him away at once, saying to him, 'See that you say nothing to anyone; but go, show yourself to the priest, and offer for your cleansing what Moses commanded, as a testimony to them. But he went out and began to proclaim it freely, and to spread the word, so that Jesus could no longer go into a town openly, but stayed out in the country; and people came to him from every quarter (Mark 1:40-45).

The Touch

Looks and words
had cut and thrown
Him out of sight
Until he too would,
If he could, have
Shunned himself.
His only power
Was to revolt
The unsuspecting
Passerby
And mock his haste
For fear of being touched.

It was just such
A seeming passing stranger
That stopped and shocked
Him with His touch,
A touch that lightly lanced
The bitter dust and shame:
A lover's, sculptor's touch

That knew of what he was created,
And dreamt of what he might,
In time, become.

Our world presents us with many tragic and touching sights. No doubt the daily news on which most of us are fed through TV, Radio and the Press is highly selective. In spite of our insatiable appetite for bad news rather than for good, the modern world actually knows very little about much of the oppression and suffering our fellow-humans have to endure. In the west often this is precisely because of its equally insatiable appetite for low-price raw materials from the 'third world'. These are the facts of life we prefer to keep out of sight. In any case, scenes of tragedy presented through TV pictures in our own living rooms as we are eating supper merely serve to make many of us ever less sensitive to the suffering of others.

The prominence of such scenes from the 'third-world' have also given westerners a ludicrously lop-sided view of that world. As well as obscene squalor, there is also so much beauty and laughter and cultural richness in third-world life. And yet, the undeserved human suffering in that life cannot be forgotten.

Leprosy was endemic in one of the areas where I lived for many years in South India. So the sight of men and women alarmingly disfigured by this disease, with face, fingers, feet ravaged almost beyond recognition as parts of a human body, sometimes with no fingers at all—lost through the repeated injuries and infection from lack of feeling—such a sight was almost a daily occurrence. And, of course, repeated exposure meant loss of sensitivity in the viewer too.

And yet, for me, perhaps the most moving scenes of my life were those, repeated each month, when a band of lepers came for whatever help we could give. The church had leprosy hospitals, in Dichpalli, in Karigiri, and in a few other places. I shall never forget playing in a cricket match against the Dichpalli team, on their delightful hospital ground, made up half of leprosy medical staff and half of treated leprosy patients. The Director was not only crazy about cricket. He was also a shrewd psychologist. And his faith in the power of cricket as therapy, as a way to boost morale among those whose self-esteem had reached zero-point, was not misplaced - judging by the joyfully competitive spirit with which those Dichpalli men played.

We also shared in the work of a clinic, on the banks of the great river Godavari, to which huge numbers came. Hindu and Christian voluntary workers together treating oozing ulcers, providing special footware and good food. And there was a leprosy settlement that the church had built. Small plots of land to work, as well as simple housing for shelter.

But this still left many who were marked by this scourge with almost nothing, unless they begged. The whole phenomenon of such begging of course raises complex questions that we will not attempt to address here. I merely describe what I saw. These leprosy sufferers had banded together, moved around from town to town, singing with a wild, desperate abandon, in their hoarse leprous voices, their songs of praise, pleading and penitence to the God they now saw as their only hope. Just seeing them bunched in song at the gate, let alone talking with them and hearing the laughs that still burst out from faces that could no longer smile — this was, every time, a moving sight.

What, then, in this story (in Mark 1:40-45) of Jesus meeting with a man marked by leprosy, is there that can help our understanding? There are some 15 million leprosy sufferers throughout the world, including surprisingly large numbers in Europe. Just think: you could fill a dozen very sizeable cities with people whose lives have been deeply scarred by this disease. Does the response of Jesus provide pointers to the way we are to respond to this reality?

I

The story begins with a leper calling out in despair to Jesus: 'If only you are willing, you can make me clean.' 'If you're willing to do anything about me. . .' He might well have said: 'If you're willing just to notice me. . .' There is, of course, that fact of our insensitivity, our being de-sensitised by so much tragedy around. But it goes further than that. Leprosy was, and still is often, so dreaded, that the leper was regarded as already as good as dead. Leprosy is so abhorrent to people that its very existence is ignored, the presence of lepers, singly or in groups, is just not recognised. Many times I have watched people walking along a city street apparently just not seeing the presence of a leper begging straight in front of them. No doubt this can be just a protective measure: 'Show the slightest interest and you'll be pestered to death. And in any case we must discourage all begging, must we not?' But it runs deeper than that.

The very term 'leper' has come to mean one who is shunned, ostracised because he is polluting, outcast because he is dangerously cursed. We are told not to use this term 'leper' any more, because it has become a term of denigration and abuse. And at least in our language we must not continue to promote this kind of alienation. In general I am sure this changing of our language is correct. But what is the reality, the actual condition of those suffering from leprosy ? They are, in many societies, still treated as outcast Lepers, as untouchables.

And why is this ? There is, of course, the common belief that leprosy is a virulently infectious disease. But it is not. 90% of people in regions where leprosy is commonly found, will be quite immune to it. In any case there is need for close and prolonged contact. Even then, there is but a small chance of becoming infected. It depends on a variety of factors; there is the immunity factor, and there are no doubt psychological factors.

Then there is the age-old fear that it is quite incurable. It is not. Diagnosed early — when the first patch of numbness appears — and treated consistently with the proper medication, a cure is almost certain, and at relatively little cost. One of my own daughters, growing up in India with us, was diagnosed as a child as having a leprous patch. She took the prescribed tablets for the required two years, and she has been perfectly well ever since.

An even worse fear is that this disease is a curse from God, or is the result of one's *karma*, the outworking of some heinous deed done in a past life. It is your *karma*, all you can do now is submit to this self-created fate. But this is not so very different from saying that God has cursed you with this dread disease because of some secret sin you must have committed. And this, probably, would have been the Jewish way of accounting for leprosy in the time of Jesus.

No wonder this leper was shouting for help from a point at some distance from Jesus. It was the law of God that compelled him to keep his distance from everyone else. Alienated from his community, he was expected to live along with the other untouchables diseased as he was. No wonder, too, this leper had such doubt about Jesus' *willingness* to try to heal him. Was he not cursed by God? What confidence could he have that Jesus would want anything to do with him? The great wonder is this leper had come to believe that somehow the wandering healer, the holy man who taught about God's new reign breaking into our lives *could* cure him if only he *would*. He did not doubt the power of Jesus; he only doubted his *will* to do so. Would Jesus *want* to? Only for those of us who, like the leper, have lost all self-esteem, have come to have a very low view of ourselves — one of the marks of the depressed state now afflicting as many as one in ten people in the West — only for such would this be the problem. Does God even want to heal us? He could if he would.

So often with us it is this unwillingness to accept ourselves, doubt as to our acceptability to God, the compelling need to try in some way to make ourselves acceptable to God, that proves the greatest obstacle to our being healed by God. For healing, we can only fall before God along with all our doubts and fears and sense of uncleanness. At this point those Indian God-lovers had it right: 'I fall before you as my only refuge, my *sharanam*'; that is the cry of the heart that truly seeks God, and will surely find healing from God.

II

The *second* feature in this story touching a leper is quite unexpected. Mark tells us (at least in very important early versions) that 'Jesus was filled with *anger*, stretched out his hand and touched him.' Other versions, of course, say that he was 'filled with pity'. Certainly Jesus healed others because of his pity, his love and compassion. And it is just because 'anger', or 'indignation' is so unexpected here, that it is probably authentic. But why this *anger*? What was Jesus indignant about?

It's very unlikely that he would express anger merely because the leper doubted his willingness. No doubt at other times he did find people's lack of response weighing heavily upon his heart. But in this case, that this leper had faith in Jesus' power to cure was a little

"FLIGHT"

miracle in itself. It is just possible that Jesus' anger was caused by the clamour and confusion, the wrong kind of fame, that would inevitably result from such a healing. To heal one who was 'as good as dead' was bound to bring people flocking for the wrong motives. And it was for this reason that Jesus tries so hard to bind this man to secrecy. Mark's Gospel gives a lot of prominence to this attempt by Jesus to keep his messianic gifts secret. And the whole question of his role as Messiah was so confused in people's minds. Maybe this lies behind the expression of anger here?

Far more likely, though, is the *inhuman state to which this leper had been reduced*. The tragic pathos of this man's life, the inhuman treatment he had to endure — this is why Jesus was angry.

There may be no expression of anger in Jyoti's 'Flight' but there is a strong sense that this man - forced into flight from human society – has been pursued by the healing Bird of Heaven (like Thompson's 'Hound of Heaven'), until finally he is caught under the Healer's wings, halted in his flight, enclosed, reassured, restored. Wings and healing rays here seem as one.

All the conditions of this leper's life were a direct contradiction of the Father's good purpose for him. Here was another human body, God's good creation, disfigured by a disease that was in no way his own doing. Here was another child of God forced to be an untouchable outcaste, compelled to wander at a distance like a scavenging dog. No wonder Jesus was angry.

It was the same kind of reason that provoked Jesus' anger at other times. When the disciples tried to stop little children from being brought for a blessing; when over-pious Pharisees condemned ordinary people as being outside the good purpose of God; when ritualist Priests prevented non-Jews from praying at the Temple, by making the Court set aside for them a market-place. These were the kinds of situations that made Jesus angry.

I noted a wayside pulpit recently: 'You can never speak the truth if you are angry.' There is, of course, an anger that is self-destructive, that is merely an expression of raging impotence, the frustration of a person unable to do anything to change a trying situation. It is an inner fire that can eat up the soul. So there is an anger in which the truth cannot be spoken.

Yet, it is often the case that *you cannot speak the truth unless you are deeply angry*. Those situations that utterly contradict the fullness of God's love for every child of his; unless these things make you angry, it is doubtful if you have seen that love, or if you can speak the truth of that love. No one is to be an untouchable. No one is to be turned away from God's kingdom because of their need, because of the brokenness of their life inflicted on them by the powerful. It is their brokenness that makes them specially eligible to be part of God's new world. This was the 'truth' that Jesus announced.

And what a powerful message this is for those once called 'untouchables' in India. 'Dalit', the 'broken ones', is the name these oppressed people now identify themselves with. No wonder Dalit leaders speak with deep anger about the still broken state of their people's life. What a powerful message to those once cruelly exploited as slaves by white Europeans. No wonder leaders of the Black People speak with anger about the still enslaved life of their people — in terms of power, money, education, social respect. Jesus — the same yesterday, today and for ever — is angry about our dehumanising ways with the powerless. We should *all* be angry; we should *all* be willing to stretch out our hand, to change things.

III

And this takes us to the *third* crucial point of this story: The touch of Jesus makes a new beginning possible. The stretched-out hands of Jesus, stretched out towards one others see as untouchable: is this not a potent image of the new life, the new world of God's reign of love, that the healings of Jesus point us towards.

In the first place the out-stretched hand makes tangible, gives embodiment to, the words of Jesus at this time: 'It is my wish to heal you. You will now be clean.' The touch of the hand is so important in so many human situations.

One of the dreadful early mistakes I made as a young missionary concerned the avoiding of human touch. I was taking services in some of the very remote villages in the huge area I'd been assigned in the Dornakal Diocese of South India. They were villages of 'outcaste' people. No one had been to this area to conduct the sacraments for a couple of years. This meant that the children Christian parents brought for baptism were in some cases well beyond infancy. They had never seen a white face, or more accurately a grey and pink face, before. I must have seemed like some terrifying ghost. And there were lines of 20 or 25 awaiting the sacramental touch. In the first village many in the line of infants and children were screaming in sheer terror within two minutes of my appearing.

The baptismal service was chaos. So I thought it less frightening for them if, instead of my taking each child into my arms, they remained in their parents arms, and I merely sprinkled them with water as the words of blessing were said. Well, it did mean that in the remaining villages the services were much more orderly. But at a sad cost. I heard later that the parents were all convinced it must be because I did not like to touch even the *children* of polluted outcaste people. I'm not sure if I was ever able completely to convince them otherwise, in the two further years I worked in that region.

The touch of his hand was not always essential to healing by Jesus. But it figures very strongly as a sign that a new beginning is now possible, that this person is welcomed by God, that healing power can flow. My friend Jyoti Sahi's pictures of Jesus not in this book usually show him with large, strong hands; his hands are prominent in an almost exaggerated way. When I asked Jyoti about this, he said: 'I don't do this consciously. But his hands point to his healing touch; his healing power touches others through his hands.' How much this untouchable leper needed the touch of Jesus' hands to convince him that he really *is* accepted by God; that he is *not* a polluted being; that he *can* be healed of his disease.

These great opposites in the human view of things — purity and pollution — figure so strongly in the social and religious history of the human race. So much of our religious ritual is meant to help us acquire a purity acceptable to God. So much of the oppression in our communities and cultures — against women, against other ethnic groups, against Black people and in India against Dalit people —

springs from a fundamental feeling that they are both polluted and polluting.

And Jesus, in this act of stretching out his hand to touch a polluted leper, shouts loud and clear that we are *wrong*; this way of thinking is against the Spirit of God; we contradict the ways of God's new world by this fear that any of God's children are polluting. 'You are clean. So go to the priest and show him that you are clean. Get him to agree that you are no longer a polluted being, so that the rest of society too can now accept you.'

IV

There is a final point to be made in this story that tells us just how much this work of Jesus in restoring the broken, in reinstating into their community those who had been outcaste, regarded as polluted — how much it *cost* Jesus. Up to this point it had been the leper who had been forced to wander in lonely places, cut off from his community. Increasingly now Jesus has to accept this lonely role. He was the 'Son of Man who had nowhere to lay his head', nowhere to be at ease and relaxed.

Mark writes that because this dramatically cured leper spread the news of Jesus' strange power, he 'could not go into a town publicly. Instead he had to stay out in lonely places; and people came to him from everywhere.' It was not only that the publicity was stirring up the wrong kind of messianic fervour. The danger was as much because he had set himself upon a path that so directly contradicted the rules of society - about who was acceptable to God and who was not; about who was pure and who was polluted; about what we should be angry about in the human community; about what kinds of people we should stretch out our hand to, that we might have some part in restoring them to the life God intends for them.

Praise the Lord, my soul;
All my being, praise his holy name.
He forgives all our sins;
He heals all our diseases.
The Lord judges in favour of the oppressed,
And restores to them their rights. (Ps 103:1-6)

5 Mob Violence

They came to the other side of the sea, to the country of the Gerasenes. And when he had stepped out of the boat, immediately a man out the tombs with an unclean spirit met him. He lived among the tombs; and no one could restrain him any more, even with a chain; for he had often been restrained with shackles and chains, but the chains he wrenched apart, and the shackles he broke in pieces; and no one had the strength to subdue him. Night and day he wandered among the tombs and hills, screaming and cutting himself with stones. When he saw Jesus from a distance, he ran and bowed down before him; and he shouted at the top of his voice, 'What have you to do with me, Jesus, Son of the Most High God? I adjure you by God, do not torment me.' For Jesus had said to him, 'Come out of the man, you unclean spirit!' Then Jesus asked him, 'What is your name?' He replied, 'My name is Mob; for we are many.' He begged him earnestly not to send them out of the country.

Now there on the hillside a great herd of pigs was feeding; and the unclean spirits begged him, 'Send us into the pigs; let us enter them.' So he gave them permission. And the unclean spirits came out and entered the pigs; and the herd, numbering about two thousand, rushed down the steep bank into the sea, and were drowned in the sea.

The pig-herders ran off and told it in the town and in the country. Then people came to see what it was that had happened. They came to Jesus and saw the demoniac sitting there, clothed and in his right mind, the very man who had the 'mob' of spirits; and they were afraid. Those who had seen what had happened to the demoniac and to the pigs reported it. Then they began to beg Jesus to leave their neighbourhood. As he was getting into the boat, the man who had been possessed by demons begged him that he might be with him. But Jesus refused, and said to him, 'Go home to your friends, and tell them how much the Lord has done for you, and what mercy he has shown you.' And he went away and began to proclaim in the region of the Ten Towns how much Jesus had done for him; and everyone was amazed. (Mark 5:1-20).

To Bear Such Pain

In different ways
We cut ourselves to pieces
Until demoniac–like
We move upon a vacant lot.
A rogue a-muck the bones,
Crushing to shards our peace of mind
Upon the jagged stones,
Howling our horror
Upon denuded hills,
Believing that
No one can bear such pain
Or breathe to make dry bones
Live whole again,
Certain that
No chain can hold.
The manic strength
That tears and pares
At raw nerve ends
And breaks and breaks
Us down.

Another crossed the waters
Unafraid !
He heard and saw
The one possessed
and still was not afraid.
He smelt the pain
And touched the cutting edge,
The drooling mouth
Of a sharply shattered mind.
He bore the lashes of the storm;
He bore our waves of panic
And bade the spineless demons flee
Below a quietened sea.
But now, as then, we beg him
To leave us and depart;
And so he also bears
A timorous, piecemeal heart.

A number of healing stories, stories pointing to peace, have moments of violence in them. None, though, have quite the violence that we find in the story of 'Mob'. It follows another violent incident: the sudden storm as the disciples took Jesus across to the other side of Lake Galilee. We're told that this lake is still subject to these fierce storms that suddenly erupt; though they are but minor spats compared to the cyclonic storms that lash such places as the south-east coast of India, where I lived for a number of years. Just a week ago the Godavari delta was again smashed by cyclonic fury and deluged by a tidal wave that claimed the lives of over 2000 people, many of them fishermen operating locally made crafts little different from those boats crossing Lake Galilee in the time of Jesus.

That Galilean storm was violent enough though.The sudden strength of the wind brought waves spilling into the boat, and there was danger of sinking. Jesus, we're told, was asleep in the stern. The frightened disciples woke him with the words, 'Don't you care that we're about to die?' Then Jesus spoke directly to the wind and to the waves, as though they were personal forces to be controlled: 'Be quiet! Be still!' Then 'there was a great calm' on the lake. It is not surprising that 'great awe' filled the hearts of the disciples. 'Who is this man', whose word can even bring peace to winds and waves, to the forces of nature?

I

It was a good lead-in to the story of Mob. The *first* thing we notice about Mob is his *alienated* state. He was out on his own, away from human habitation, living in the burial caves. He identified himself with the dead, not with the living. Perhaps he felt he communicated with the spirits of the dead; perhaps he heard the inner voices of schizophrenia, and identified these with the spirits of the dead who were all around him. He certainly could no longer communicate with his own contemporaries. Their most recent attempts to relate to him had been by way of tying him down with chains, trying to keep him fettered, probably in some dark dungeon-like inner room, away from the rest of society. He was someone to be hidden from the sight of normal people — a shame to his family. They no doubt *wanted* to alienate him, probably giving up very early on any attempt to communicate with this 'madman' they were cursed with.

What really were the causes of Mob's alienation? We do not know any such background details. What we do know is that people labelled as 'mad', and in many societies treated inhumanly, are often merely *different*. They may not conform to what most of us see as 'normal'. But that is not necessarily dangerous 'madness'. Why, Jesus too was called 'mad'; just as was the nineteenth century Indian saint, Ramakrishna, and the prophet Muhammad in seventh century Arabia. In 'modern' societies we usually like to keep those we see as a little too abnormal under permanent sedation in secure institutions. But then we go to the opposite extreme of releasing such people into the community with inadequate care-structures; and tragedies occur from time to time, further increasing the fear of the 'normal'.

II

Secondly, it is clear that Mob was a person in great *inner torment*. He sees himself as already as good as dead. 'He wandered among the tombs and hills, screaming and cutting himself with stones.' There is more loud screaming when Jesus approaches: 'For God's sake, I beg you, don't punish me.' And yet there is that constant painful self-mutilation, self-punishment. As noted above, of the root-cause of the inner conflict that lies behind all this we have no clue. But this often seems to be the case with that broad range of mental sickness we call schizophrenia. A loss of inner control and equilibrium, a disintegration at the centre of the self, a sense of being taken over by some alien force, quite suddenly develops in those who until then may have seemed fairly ordinary people. But then the *inner torment*. And all so unpredictable.

In the Day Centre for those recovering from this and other forms of mental illness that was part of the community work of the inner-city Leicester church I ministered in recently for six years, there was frequent opportunity to talk with, and sometimes pray with, sometimes just sit with, men and women who feared they were, or had been, in the grip of some other power. The medication they took of course dulled the intensity of their feelings. But what struck me so often was the *inner torment* they had to endure every day — perhaps especially those with religious faith, however much that faith also helped to give them the courage and hope to struggle on.

The inner torment of the man in this story is all too clear. On the one hand he comes 'running' to meet Jesus, almost as though he is looking eagerly for healing; and he recognises the power in this stranger, power to restore the inner peace he so desperately needed. On the other hand he pleads with Jesus to leave him alone, not to 'torment' or 'punish' him. The inner loss of integration, and the subsequent self-torment, are obvious.

III

A *third*, very obvious, feature of Mob's character, is the *violence*. A small number of those we call 'schizophrenic' can, and sometimes tragically do, carry out acts of seriously destructive violence. Mob's violent acts were directed at himself. Part of his fractured personality wanted to wound, mutilate, punish, destroy *himself*. Other parts of that fractured self were saying, 'Assert yourself, be aggressive.' He was a self-divided person, perhaps even a multiple personality. When Jesus asked him his name, he answered: 'My name is "Mob", there are so many of us.' 'Legion' is the name that most English translations give this inwardly tormented man. And the original Greek actually uses the same word. But the Good News Bible's 'Mob' far more accurately expresses this man's disturbed inner self, the violent inner conflict, the unpredictable behaviour as he was torn by opposing forces. None of this suggests the ordered power of a military legion.

A more important question, though, in this context is: How much of the wounding we receive in life is in fact 'self-inflicted'? Do we do justice to ourselves constantly to be blaming *others*, the traumas they have caused us, for the inner conflicts we have to cope with and the inadequacies we experience? Since Freud, parents have been seen as the main culprits in this regard; they have almost been demonised in much psycho-therapy. What is important, though, is not merely identifying the causes of wounding to the fragile psyche of our early years. Many parents *are* in fact dangerously inadequate - in part no doubt because their own parents were, and so on back to Adam and Eve.

In other words, inadequacy and imperfection mark the way our world is. It is within this context that we are to struggle for healthier inner being. Part of that struggle is to recognise the traumas that were inflicted on us - perhaps by parents, perhaps by teachers who indulged in the fierce caning of the children in their care, maybe because they sincerely believed this to be the only way properly to care for children; maybe because they just lost self-control, or perhaps found perverted pleasure in whipping little children. I personally was subjected to violent caning by both kinds of teachers, at primary school and at boarding school. It is the psyche that suffers more even than the physical pain.

We do need to probe the trauma-points in our early development. But we also need to engage in a healthy self-critical examining of the many ways we too inflict wounds on *others*, and how we inflict wounds on *ourselves*. It is so often said that those who were abused as children — psychologically, physically, sexually — go on to abuse others. It is this kind of literally vicious cycle that we have to break out of — if we are to share in the healing work, in the kind of healing life, to which Jesus points us.

We do violence to others in so many different ways, sometimes very subtle ways, sometimes very crude. Mention was made above of the violent storms on the south-east Indian coast. On the Krishna delta, slightly further south than the Godavari area where the recent tragedy occurred, I remember seeing a memorial to two or three English people who were drowned in just such a tidal wave around 100 years ago. At the bottom of the impressively carved stone, in tiny script, there is mention of the seemingly incidental fact that some 20, 000 local 'natives' also perished in the storm.

There is a form of violence, far more destructive than the cyclonic tidal wave, expressed in that monument's superscription. For behind it lies the 200 years of insidious violence done by the British to the Indian psyche as well as to the physical resources of the country. This shameful history is something both British and Indian people have to reckon with in understanding themselves, and for the 'healing' they both need. With such healing awareness, both now need to move beyond that history. We all need to become aware of the damage to our wholeness of being we *inflict upon ourselves*.

Some ways of being violent in our treatment of others is subtle and unseen, yet can be even more dangerous than open physical blows. Our search for peace, therefore, the peace which is the deep desire and prayer of every heart, must never focus only on the obvious ways of being violent. Such a peace, when there is no probing to the deeper wounds that people bear, can prove to be a mere covering over of the most dangerous types of violence we inflict on one another. Any search for peace that ignores issues of deeper injustice done — perhaps to those who themselves seem to be acting violently — will be just such a cover-up. *Facing up to all the demons within us, and to the self-contradictions within us, is a key part of the healing process*. This is precisely what Jesus expected from this violently tormented 'Mob', when he asked him his name. Even if there are times when it seems inevitable that some kind of violence has to precede peace, the wholeness of life that is true peace, true *shalom*, is always threatened by that violence by which we wound either others or ourselves.

The ancient Indian concept of *jiva-ahimsa*, or 'non-injury to creatures', without any doubt, has made a very significant impact on human history. Far beyond Indian cultural life, large parts of Asia and important figures in modern global history — especially Martin Luther King and Nelson Mandela, influenced by Mahatma Gandhi — have been moved by this vision of non-violence as the only true way, the only possible way, for the human race. As all these leaders have seen, such an ethic of non-violence is closely in tune with both the sayings and the life-style of Jesus.

And yet, whether in India, or America, or South Africa, it is so easy to allow this theory of non-violence to become a protective screen hiding the reality of countless forms of violence against oppressed people we so earnestly urge to remain non-violent as they struggle for a new life. In the end, of course violence can only breed further violence. But at least there has to be a far more open-eyed awareness by would-be Gandhians (like myself?) of just how much violence, both open and hidden, the poor have to put up with before we begin our exhortations to them to be non-violent in their response. Healing is not possible without realism, even if realism leads nowhere without a vision of the new future that God intends for us.

IV

There is a *fourth* development in this story of Mob that has strange, even violent, features. At the time of Mob's healing, 2000 pigs grazing nearby suddenly take off, rush down the cliff-face, and drown themselves in the lake. There are commentators who have tried to rationalize what happened. It was Mob's violence and screaming at the time of his demons being exorcised that frightened the pigs into this self-destructive flight. Perhaps so. But the story itself wants us to link their drowning more closely than that with the demons' destruction. And Mob's new-found wholeness is shown as dependent on the pigs' drowning. The story even tells of the demons negotiating this exit with Jesus, for they feared he would send them too far away, away to oblivion. To inhabit the lake was a far more acceptable destiny for them it seems. For the waters of the Lake were seen as the home of the forces of chaos, as the sudden violent storm preceding Mob's healing had shown. But perhaps it was really Mob who needed some form of tangible evidence that his demons were banished. And pigs, of course, were seen as fatally unclean animals, not an acceptable part of God's creation. So, for Mob to identify his banished demons and the doomed pigs was very natural. Equally natural was the alarm of the pig-grazers. When I lived in Dornakal in the shadow of the indigenously styled Cathedral of the Epiphany, built by Bishop Azariah, the first Indian to become an Anglican Bishop, most of the small hamlets scattered around nearby were inhabited by people of different tribes. The Erukalas were one of them, a pig-grazing people. They loved their animals, and each year at Harvest Festival would carry some of their pigs into the Cathedral, right up to the sanctuary, for the Bishop's blessing. There is no reason to think the pig-keepers in the Mob-story loved their pigs any less. In any case, their economy depended on them. No wonder they ask Jesus to leave their region.

"SERPENT CHAINED"

So there are serious questions to be asked in connection with Mob's healing. Would Jesus deliberately destroy the resources by which these people lived? Even if Mob's healing depended on it? Would Jesus assume that one man's wholeness is worth the life of 2000 pigs — apart from the matter of their owners' livelihood? Sometimes there are questions we just do not have answers to. Or maybe those who rationalise the drowning of the pigs, in line with what we know of Jesus from other stories, are right here.

But the closing scene is impressive. People from all around came to see what had happened to this man they'd believed to be permanently mad. And there he was sitting with Jesus, 'clothed and in his right mind'. Wearing the clothes expected by others around is in itself a sign that we share their world, their culture, their life; we're one with them. Mob was 'home' again. If this impressed and delighted people, it also filled them with an awe towards Jesus that made them want to keep him at some distance. His powers, they felt, were too uncanny, too unpredictable, for it to be safe with him around. So, again, they ask him to leave.

Mob was eager to go with him. But Jesus sees his role as that of a witness in his own place, among his own people: 'Go back home to your family and tell them how much the Lord has done for you.' Right here is where your home is, where previously you were violent, destructive, unable to relate to others. Right here is the place to tell of the goodness of God, the healing purpose of God, the in-breaking of God's power to make wounded and fractured selves whole as you have found through Jesus. Here is the place to be at home, the place to be whole within yourself, the place to build up new forms of wholeness with your people.

Jyoti's 'Serpent Chained' suggests that the healing of the extreme violence and related traumas of disturbed Mob calls for a burning up, a rising up from the old ashes, Phoenix-like, into flames of new life. And it is the Healer who is aflame, aflame with passion, holding close to his heart the struggling figure of the 'demon-possessed', a figure entwined with a writhing snake, the ancient deadly enemy of the bird. Death, then, as well as the distress of our life, is overcome in the heavenly Bird's fire of love.

6 Wailing for a Sleeping Child

When Jesus had crossed again in the boat to the other side, a great crowd gathered around him; and he was by the sea. Then one of the leaders of the synagogue named Jairus came and, when he saw him, fell at his feet and begged him repeatedly, 'My little daughter is at the point of death. Come and place your hands on her, so that she made be made well, and live.' So he went with him. And a large crowd followed and pressed in on him... some people came from the leader's house to say, 'Your daughter is dead. Why trouble the teacher any further?' But overhearing what they said, Jesus said to the leader of the synagogue, 'Do not fear, only believe.' He allowed no one to follow him except Peter, James, and John, the brother of James. When they came to the house of the leader of the synagogue, he saw the confusion and heard all the loud wailing and crying. When he had entered, he said to them, 'Why all this confusion and weeping? The child is not dead but sleeping.' And they laughed at him. Then he put them all outside, and took the child's father and mother and those who were with him, and went in where the child was. He took her by the hand and said to her, 'Talitha cum,' which means, 'Little girl, get up!' And immediately the girl got up and began to walk about (she was twelve years of age). At this they were overcome with amazement. He strictly ordered them that no one should know this, and told them to give her something to eat (Mark 5:21-24, 35-43).

Drawn Back from the Edge

The girl was at the edge
Of womanhood, a prey
To change and passing mood,
Mind and body moving
At uneven and unaccustomed paces.
She felt a tide that overran
And then drew back

Draining her to sleep.
The clamour ebbed
And in the lull
His quiet voice flowed
Down to her confusion
And she awoke hungry
To re-live.

It is the *setting* for the acts of healing in Jesus' ministry that often is so important. It may be the wild caves of Gadara, or the pilgrim road from Jericho, or the healing pool of Bethesda, or a Synagogue on the Sabbath. It's the milieu that often gives meaning to the healing; the atmosphere around that often adds to its significance.

Today's story is that of the healing of the little daughter of Jairus, a Galilean Synagogue official. Mark sets the scene skilfully, for all the roughness of his style generally. Things were happening fast in this Gospel.

I

In fact, that is the first *feature of this story* that we shall take note of—the *confusion and the urgency around Jesus*. From its beginning with the preaching of John the Baptist, the first three chapters of Mark are action-packed, most incidents prefaced by 'as soon as' or 'at once', as though everything is intensely urgent; then there's a more tranquil batch of seed-and-harvest parables; then we're into this section, with the quietening of the stormy winds and waves, his calming of the wild ravings and self-destructive violence of 'Mob' of Gadara; then Jesus is back across the Lake, and 'there at the lakeside a large crowd gathered round him', begging for his attention.

Among them is Jairus, with his passionate plea as he threw himself at the feet of Jesus: 'My little daughter is very ill. Please come and place your hands upon her, so that she will be well and live.' So much passion and pathos, not only in this story, but in several others too where parents plead for their children. People cannot understand why their children should have to suffer. These are real, raw, urgent human emotions that the Gospel depicts for us as the setting for Jesus' healing acts. The human situation is very real here.

People's confusion comes across in various ways. They 'crowd in on him from every side', as we noted. But they are all persons with very different needs, not just 'the crowd'. And one of them takes this chance, with the crowd around, to 'touch the hem of his cloak' as a way of healing her long-endured haemorrhaging. More pathos, more confusion. And in this case, another healing, another blessing for wholeness of life: 'My daughter, go in peace'. But we take up her story after this one about the daughter of Jairus.

And this feeling of urgency is in the crowd's behaviour too. They 'press upon him', 'crowd around him from every side'. There is clamour and confusion. And we have conflicting accounts of her condition. She's very ill; she's dead; she's sleeping. Only halfway to the house, and Jesus feels it necessary to keep his followers at a distance from such a confused situation, except for the inner three — Peter, James, John. The others were not yet ready for the turmoil of it all. And when they reach the home of Jairus and the little girl? 'Jesus saw the confusion and heard all the loud crying and wailing. . . "Why all this confusion? Why this crying?"

At first it seems as though Jesus *adds* to the confusion. 'The child is not dead. She is only sleeping.' And their response is what anyone would expect. 'They laughed at him.' Surely they knew a dead child when they saw one! Their ridicule is natural enough. Perhaps they even felt that it was cruel on Jesus' part to raise the parents' hopes in this crude way. A child that is dead is dead, not just 'sleeping'. And if it's meant as a gentle euphemism, it's just not facing the awful finality of death.

So the mourners, perhaps professional wailers as some suggest, laugh at him. Why there should be professional mourners, though, is doubtful. In such a death-scene anywhere in the East, there would be plenty of family members freely and forcefully expressing their feelings of grief. The hiding of grief, thinking tears something to be ashamed of, has never been part of eastern culture. Even Jesus' act of removing such mourners from the scene would have added to the turmoil and chaos.

The scene around this little girl, then, as Jesus enters the house, is very confused and chaotic. But this is exactly how things are in the world. Of course there are countless little oases of peaceful homes and places of quiet. The world as a whole, though, is a place of clamour, of crowding, of crying, of conflict.

Even our homes are just not the places of orderly peace that we would like them to be. Just where we would expect there should be gentleness and calm, behind the facade there may well be hidden violence, fear and confusion. And the same is true within our places of care for children, even Christian institutional Homes. All over the world it has come to light in the past few years that in dozens of such Homes, those given the task of caring for needy children have, even if only a small minority of such carers, too often been sexually abusing them. A recent report in Britain makes an even more damning claim: it is said that among 'ordinary' families as many as a million children are abused — either sexually, or by some form of violence. And this in the very places we would most expect to find gentleness and peace.

It is a similar story on a wider scale. Four places in the world where I have enjoyed periods of inner healing and peace are the tiny 'Paradise Island' of Sri Lanka, the beautiful Vale of Kashmir, the 'Emerald Isle' that is Ireland, the wonderful mountain kingdom of Nepal. Nepal is quiet again, and the areas of 'the troubles' in Ireland are relatively small. But all these places of delight, and many more, have known horrifying violence for which solutions seem so elusive. And more often than not it is children who suffer the greatest traumas from the violence around them.

There are, of course, other ways of being violent to children and causing irreparable confusion to their so easily traumatised psyches. Two recent statistics scream out countless sad stories. The International Labour Organisation has just told us that more than 250 million children are now working, usually very long hours, often under appalling conditions, in mining, construction, mills, factories, agriculture, fishing and domestic service. Small children as young as *three* are regularly used in India's fire-work and match factories. This is economic exploitation at its worst, even if it merely reflects the global fact of the economic within which the 'third world' is held by its 'developed' global partners. The second statistic relates to the sex trade. At least one million children in Asia alone are now bought and sold each day as rising numbers are forced into child prostitution and child pornography. Just imagine what violence this kind of life does to the vulnerable psyches of young children.

But this is how the world is. We would *like* to shut it all out, just not think about it lest it disturb our peace of mind. But such is *not the way of Jesus.* He walks straight into places where there is clamour and confusion, weeping and wailing, and the genuine pathos of mourning. He accepts the reality of it, and the depth of our suffering. And he challenges the confusion of our world: 'Why?' It is not necessary that your world be so. It can be very different. *Why* is there violence? *Why* is there the age-old injustice that is the root-cause of this violence? *Why* do you persist in such destructive ways of life? 'Why all this confusion?'

II

The *second* key-feature of this story is the *human concern* we find in it. There is the natural concern of the father, who forgets the dignity of his position as an ecclesiastical official, and 'threw himself at the feet of Jesus'. We've already noted the passion and pathos in his pleading: 'Please come. . . that my little daughter may be made well and live.' There is no more intense emotion than that felt by a caring parent when their child's life is threatened. And this fact of parental concern—often only maternal concern of course — is deeply embedded in the instincts of the whole animal kingdom.

No scene in the natural world is more hideously gruesome than that of a seething pack of vultures feeding with gluttonous and squabbling ferocity from the dead carcase of a buffalo. And yet, when you watch those same vultures feeding tiny titbits to their young ones, you see a miracle of maternal gentleness and concern. It is precisely because this parental instinct — to care for children no matter what the cost—is so deep in our human nature that the abusing of children is such a shockingly unnatural evil.

In a number of the healing stories, the concern of parents for their children, of families for their loved ones, of others for their friends, is an essential part of the process of healing. Jesus accepts and respects people's concern for those they love. In the case of one parent who had come about his child, at first Jesus seems discouraged that no one is interested in what he has to say, only in the signs and wonders. But the father in that story immediately shows that his concern is very simple: 'Please come before my child dies'. In the case of the brother of Mary and Martha, Jesus even weeps with them over his death. He shares with us the pain of loving.

In our present story, it is true, he seems at first to treat rather brusquely and unfeelingly those mourning the death of the little girl. But in this case there was the need for calm and quiet in the inner room, as Jesus took only the mother and father, along with his closest disciples, to ensure the girl's recovery. Again, the presence of those most deeply concerned for her was part of her recovery.

Our natural human concerns and feelings, then, are accepted by God as an essential part of our life as we seek God's healing at all points in that life. Feelings are not the *only* reality, as some counsellors seem to suggest. But they certainly are crucial. It is crucial that we find what our deepest feelings and concerns really are. We need that sort of inner awareness, if there is to be healing. No doubt our natural concerns also need the transforming touch, however gradual its effect. There may be too much anger, too much anxiety, too much selfishness in our concern. Mothering can become unhealthy smothering. Or our concern, being natural, may be too exclusively focused on our own loved ones. And we need to move on, to enlarge these natural feelings so that we learn to embrace God's wider family.

Our concerns need to share more and more in God's concern. And this too is one of the aims of the healing Jesus brings about. Should this not also be a central aim in all our praying, and in our approaching God for healing? That our natural concerns grow to overlap and be in tune with God's concerns?

And there is a delightful detail mentioned as following the recovery of the girl. There is the usual 'strict order' not to tell anyone. No doubt this was part of the great problem of people misunderstanding what his mission was all about. Large tomes have been written about this 'messianic secret'. But here there is also the negative effect such publicity could have upon this little girl. They must try to protect her from such public fervour. And the closing word is another clue to the down-to-earthness of Jesus' concern for her. 'Give her something to eat.' Whatever the experience she'd been through, it was an ordeal. She now needed some food, something nutritious to hasten a full recovery.

And this raises an issue that is so crucial to health: good food for children. On the one hand many millions are cruelly deprived of any food, and die either from starvation, or from disease to which they become vulnerable because their families cannot give them the food they need. The suffering of parents watching this is as great as that of the children who die.

In far more cases than not, such starvation is the result, direct or indirect, of policies and practices of those who wield power and control the destinies of the world's starving. These may be governments *within* the country concerned, or global powers outside the direct control of that country. But for the world's well-fed to say resignedly, as most of us do, 'What a pity, but nothing can be done', is an obscenity, even if the redistribution of global resources, education in community health, the controlling of global population, the pursuing of ecologically sustainable production and economic policies, are interwoven issues of great complexity. That these issues are not easily resolvable does not make our acceptance of them any less morally obscene.

Most morally obscene, of course, is the fact that in the one global village that our world is rapidly becoming, alongside the starving children are those who do not eat well because of the excess of fast-foods, snacks, choc-bars, candies, and general junk-food pressed upon them continually in the consumer-driven arena our children's world has become. It is the future health and well-being of our children that is at stake here.

Junk-food is not the only problem unfortunately. There is, for example, the long-standing campaign by the manufacturers of baby foods to persuade third-world mothers to change from breast-feeding to their own tinned baby-foods. As a supplement when there is need, of course, baby-foods can be wonderful. But when, in spite of

"SWAN'S CRY"

binding agreements to the contrary, baby-food companies still feed misinformation to third-world mothers, thereby persuading them to give up breast-feeding, the churches are quite right to threaten those companies again (as they have done this week) with further boycotting. Even more serious for the future is the probability of increased genetic engineering of food, along with the effects of pesticides and other poisonous substances regularly pumped into some stage of the food-chain. We just do not know what may yet happen to human health as a result of these and other new forms of artificial food-production. But it is our children who will suffer. We should be thankful that there seem to be a growing number of people — in Britain, India, Germany, America, and elsewhere — who are becoming aware of these issues and are prepared to speak out. 'Give (our children) something good to eat.'

Then there may well be yet another kind of meaning in these considerate words of Jesus. Those who are raised from death to life, following the uplifting touch of Jesus, are also promised the nurture they need for their continuing journey of faith. In ecclesial terms - after the new life offered in baptism, there is the feeding at the Lord's Table. Either way, the unfailing *concern* of Jesus for his children's well-being is a strong feature in his healing ministry.

In Jyoti's 'Swan's Cry' the 'concern' of Jesus almost reverses the roles here. It is the healing Bird who lifts her head, like a mother calling to God in anguish for her child's life, yet still covering the child with the overarching wings of a mother. The Healer becomes the wailer, such is his heart of compassion. And the child, her mother beside her, lies 'asleep', trapped in a seed-like cocoon, as though awaiting new wings.

III

And so to the *third* feature of this story of the healing of Jairus' daughter. Countering the confusion, and challenging the concern, there is the *conviction* of Jesus. His calm certainty first emerges clearly when they arrive from Jairus' house with the message, 'Your daughter is dead. Why bother the Teacher any more?' The response of Jesus seems to ooze calm conviction, even though it counters all the evidence so far: 'Don't be afraid; only believe.' These words echo his chiding of the disciples a little earlier when the stormy waves were calmed: 'Why are you afraid? Where is your faith?' And in most of the healing stories, *faith* is seen as the key to finding the healing power of God. In one such story — the Healing of the Epileptic Son — Jesus even says, 'Everything is possible to those who believe.' Just what this means we shall look at more closely when we come to that story.

Clearly it does *not* mean literally anything at all is possible, even if it *does* mean that our understanding of, and response to, any situation of suffering is to be governed by the outward evidence. We are *never* to be guided by our fear of how things look. We are *never* to assume that suffering and death are the last word. We are never to lose the hope that God's purpose for his children is that they be healed, however bleak the immediate outlook may appear.

When I took up a ministry in Leicester in 1988 I was introduced to John, already almost paralysed by Multiple Sclerosis. By nature John was a very active sort, a bit of a comedian, always ready with some witty response. When his MS was well-advanced, it wasn't always like that at home, of course. There were times there when his frustration got the better of him, for all his deep love for his wife and two adolescent children. John attended a healing group a couple of times a week. There was often some slight improvement after a session with the healing group. But speech had become distressingly difficult. Even so, he was still saying: 'I know that I'm going to be healed. In fact, it's my faith that God has already healed me', though you often had to listen very hard to make out the meaning. Of course there were low-mood times also when he spoke of his fear. But his fear and distress did not determine his whole outlook. One part of him knew quite well he was going to die; he had already almost died several times. Yet his faith was in the healing that he also knew was God's purpose for him. Indeed, inner healing was taking place already; though in his case the fullness of God's healing had to wait for the world of God's eternity. And that's what we celebrated at his funeral, remembering the wit and the faith, and commending him to the life of fullness yet to come.

Conviction about God's purpose for us, then — the conviction that it is not God's purpose that little children suffer and die — is an essential part of the healing process. So Jesus enters that house in which there was such fear and panic, as well as the natural pain and distress of family and friends, and challenges the mourners with his new perception of the little girl's condition. 'Why all this confusion? She is not dead; she is only sleeping.'

Jesus put a lot of why-questions to his followers and to others. Now it's our turn to put such a question. Why speak of this child, believed dead by her relatives, as 'only sleeping'? Explaining it as some have done, in terms of a coma, mistaken as death by her family, is definitely not the meaning Mark intends. Extreme as the claim may seem, the Gospel-story is that Jesus raises people 'from death to life'; that Jesus brings into the human situation, with all its confusion of life and death, of hope and fear, of joy and pain, such potential for healing that, in the end, even death — that last and fiercest of our enemies — is overcome.

The word 'con-viction' comes from 'together overcoming'. It's no trivial detail in this story that Jesus takes the two parents and his three closest disciples along with him into the place where this little girl lay. However much at this stage Jesus was alone in his 'conviction', in his faith in God's healing purpose, his intention is that others share with him in the 'overcoming'. Similarly their natural 'concern' is to become one with his wider, God-tuned concern, using this term too in its literal meaning, 'discerning with'.

Along with Jesus, his followers also were yet to 'discern' that this most terrifying fact of our humanness, the surest sign of our mortality, *can* be seen as if we are 'only sleeping'. Such discernment in no way lessens death's reality. No one is to think that death, as some spiritualities try to teach us, is unreal. Death is as real as life; earth is as real as heaven. So Jesus' conviction that death is a 'sleep' means that death is not the last word about life. It is not the end of all hope and meaning. However traumatic the loss of life, healing, even in death, is possible — is in fact promised.

So, then, the confidence of Jesus was in the loving, powerful purpose of God: whatever the girl's state, she will wake up; there's new life awaiting her; there's hope for God's children even in their darkest hours: 'Little girl, rise up from your sleep.' And the original Aramaic words, *Talitha, kum*, are retained, showing just how important these words were for the faith of the followers of Jesus long after he had died and risen and ascended. They too came to share fully in this *conviction* of Jesus, that suffering and death are not the last word.

In the end, then, our ability to come to terms with death will depend upon the degree of healing we experience in life; it will depend upon the value we place upon life itself, and how far we remove those factors in our life together that make for destruction and violence and death. The chaos and confusion that typifies the social worlds we have made for ourselves can be overcome, even though the act of addressing and confronting our confused and disordered lives may well at first entail even more confusion — as was the case with Jesus. And to talk of healing even in death, and of overcoming death, will no doubt cause plenty of laughter among those for whom such faith and hope is a nonsense. Yet this is the faith and the hope to which the followers of Jesus are to witness.

7 The Woman at the Edge of Things

A large crowd followed him and pressed in on him. Now there was a woman who had been suffering from haemorrhaging for twelve years. She had suffered terribly under many physicians, and had spent all that she had; and she was no better, but rather grew worse. She had heard about Jesus, and came up behind him in the crowd and touched the edge of his cloak, for she said, 'If I only touch his clothes, I will be made well.' Immediately her haemorrhage stopped; she felt in her body that she was healed of her disease. Immediately aware that power had gone out of him, Jesus turned about in the crowd and said, 'Who touched my clothes?' And his disciples said to him, 'You see the crowd pressing in on you; how can you say, "Who touched me?"' Jesus looked all around to see who had done it. But the woman, knowing what had happened to her, came in fear and trembling, fell down before him, and told him the whole truth. Jesus said to her, 'Daughter, your faith has made you whole; go in peace, and be healed of your disease.' (Mark 5:24-34).

'Who Touched Me'?

Relieved to be unknown, unshunned
In the clamour of the crowd's tide
She was shoved, elbowed, pressed
From each unsuspecting side
Nearer, nearer to be blessed.

For twelve plagued years
While others ripened, she decayed,
Festered by blood's flow
And hardened tears,
Her womanhood repelled.
She was disgraced, displaced
And her outraged spirit rebelled
At the fear of unpatterned chaos
She unleashed.

In her own way
She had struggled to be healed,
Surrendering wealth, sense, pride
Submitting to outlandish promised cures
Of men unbothered if she died;
She had knocked, hammered, kicked,
Waged war - at God's unyielding door.

Now,
The crowd around her seethed and sank;
She stood, no one between, unseen,
Afraid to stand full face to face
But sure she was alone and one with Him.

She dared to claim that even she
Was not cast out beyond God's grace;
Her hand stretched out to touch
Just woven cloth - and she received,
Her trembling faith at last believed.

Few of the healing stories of Jesus are so pregnant with insight as this one, the story of the woman who touched the edge of his cloak. No wonder it figures prominently in the writing of feminist interpreters. There are so many clues for better understanding the situation of women through the ages, including our own. And it tells us so much about the healing that is God's purpose for us.

I

She is *first* described as a 'woman who had suffered terribly'. In her case the cause of this suffering was very specific: she had some kind of chronic haemorrhaging, and so was weakened continually by this loss of blood. The word used for her complaint is 'scourge'; it is as though she was being painfully punished, whipped mercilessly, undeservedly, as Jesus was.

Studies have shown that women generally suffer far more than men in life; and yet at least in western society they remain inherently stronger than men, medically and mentally, and live longer.

Where women are still expected to go on bearing more and more children, with little respite between births, and where they do not enjoy a diet that will counter this, their health suffers tragically, whatever may be their inherent strength. The wife in a number of societies is the 'one who carries', if not children, then other loads. She is a load-bearer. Scenes from all over the globe show us women as the ones with the load on their head, their hip, their back. Sometimes men share this load, often not. And I've not yet even mentioned the excruciating pain of child-labour.

As the 'carrier', the woman is also the primary *carer*; and this is her role in most cultures. Not just the one who is to care for her children; the woman is also expected to care for the life of the home — cooking, washing, cleaning — as well as care for the sick and the elderly. To a large extent this is true of the woman's given role in wider society too, not only in her own house. In general it is women who are expected to be cleaners, nurses, housekeepers, and suchlike; and are then rewarded with the minimum possible pay.

Add to this the fact that it is still usual, even where a woman works outside the home, to expect her to carry out all family-caring and house-caring duties as well; which means that a woman in modern society may well be doing two or even three jobs to her man's one. Is it any wonder that women are twice as likely to experience depressive illness, whatever may be women's inherent mental strength? Yet in most societies today they still manage to live, on average, five years longer than men. And even this prolonged widowhood — given a happy marriage — adds further to the suffering a woman can expect, whatever her greater ability to cope with loneliness.

The woman who came to Jesus had 'suffered terribly'; in this she was not greatly different from many of her sex through the ages. They have been made to feel the 'scourge'.

And there are other, specific reasons for this woman's suffering, and for wanting to stay on the edge of the crowd, to touch but the edge of the cloak of Jesus. In the *first* place she suffered from a great *sense of shame*. This is why she does not feel able to approach Jesus directly; her complaint is one that she would not want talked about publicly, though we do not know precisely the nature of her 'issue of blood', to use the older translation. In any case probably very few even of her friends will have been told about it. Women often tend to keep these things to themselves. And very probably those older women in the family who did know about it, had made her feel deep shame about it. No doubt they had said she must have done something secretly evil to have brought this on herself. Sickness of this kind the world over is interpreted in this judgemental way. It is a 'scourge' that for some secret reason must have been deserved.

Such feelings of shame, of course, closely relate to the general sense of *impurity* women in many cultures are made to feel, just because they are women. It is precisely their monthly blood, and their child-bearing, their whole sexuality, for which men have seen them as impure, as a great threat. During menstruation, in many traditional societies, they have to live apart from others, perhaps even outside the house. Then, if at any time a sexual misdemeanour occurs between a man and a woman, it is the *woman* who will be blamed, even though she has been brought up to believe she must always be obedient to men. So often there is great fear of women's sexuality; the woman is seen as by nature dangerously seductive, voraciously sexual, and all this must be rigorously curbed.

Nor is this just the fevered repressions of those of strict Protestant faith, as some seem to imagine. For all the ills of modernity — and there are many — at least there is less pressure on women to feel ashamed of being a woman. Except in those churches — Catholic, Orthodox and still some Anglican — that bar women from the priesthood. Some Evangelicals are even more anti-women: they bar them from any public ministry, based on the judgement of Paul, which merely reflected the cultural life of his time, that 'women should not speak in public', for it would bring shame upon her. And this woman who came to Jesus was clearly burdened with a sense of shame.

II

Secondly, she came as a vulnerable person who had been *exploited*. The story tells us that 'she had been treated by many doctors. (And) she had spent all her money; but instead of getting better, she got worse all the time.' Well, perhaps they had genuinely tried to cure her. The Hippocratic oath is not always a cover for the hypocritic art of medical quackery. There are, and probably always have been, countless good doctors. The fact is, though, that there have always been doctors — and lawyers, and politicians, and builders, and teachers, and clergy, and members of all professions — who have used their position, their power, their specialist knowledge, to exploit and dupe those dependent upon them.

In Indian history the Guru has been a crucial figure in the development of cultural and spiritual life. And yet, even the Guru, with his secret skills and knowledge, has sometimes exploited his authority quite unscrupulously. And, once more, it is women who are often the victims of such exploitation.

Economic exploitation of the powerless, male or female, is of course rampant globally. But women have been economic fodder in quite cunning ways. Globally women perform a huge segment of the work the human race does day by day. Yet women are officially listed as one *third* of the total workforce. Their income weighs in at one *tenth* of the total human wage. And their property is one *hundredth* of total global property. In a country like Britain, where there are supposed to be equal opportunities and equal pay for women and men, the reality is quite different, as many women are economically forced to work in shops and mills for far lower wages than men, and as fewer and fewer are taken on as permanent workers.

But there is a far more evil exploitation of the bodies of women. One form of this, obviously, is prostitution. When the women are paid well, we can be misled into thinking that at least this is not *economic* exploitation, however devoid of respect for the woman. The reality is, though, that millions of women throughout the world drift into prostitution, are often *sold* into prostitution, from sheer poverty. And the vast majority in any case remain virtually the slave of their pimps and brothel keepers.

And if prostitution is an evil, at least in part, because there is no *respect* for the woman's body (called the 'holy temple of the Spirit of God' by the Apostle) — no respect for the woman, no respect by the woman — then the *rape* of women, and the widespread violence against the bodies of women, is the ultimate act of contempt, evil contempt. The rape of women, and the deliberate mutilation of women's bodies, was probably the most horrific feature of the 'ethnic cleansing' practised systematically in Bosnia recently, mainly (though not exclusively) by Serb forces against Bosnian Muslims. It was meant as an ultimate act of contempt, for women, as well as for the race they represented.

The same violent contempt through rape is meted out to the women of Dalit communities in India by men of the 'higher' caste land-owning groups when they feel threatened by the new movements for freedom among these erstwhile 'untouchables'. 'Dalit', the 'broken people', is the name they now give themselves as they seek a new corporate identity. The women of these 'untouchables' are the 'twice-broken'.

But there are other, more 'respectable', ways of exploiting women's bodies. In some societies, women's bodies are used mainly as the instrument for perpetuating the *male* line. Is this not what males fight about so fiercely in most of the animal world? Females are but necessary repositories for the male seed. And if she is unable to produce a son, she is worthless. If this woman who came to Jesus in fact had a menstrual problem, was this the major agony that lay behind her quest for healing? She could not satisfy her husband? She could not supply him with an heir?

There is a widespread lust for male progeny. From the moment a girl child is born in many societies, there is a good chance she will be made to sense she is unwanted. Many thousands each year are not even given that chance: they are destroyed at birth. With the development of the means to find out if the foetus is male or female, hundreds of thousands of females are being aborted. In India and China the male-female imbalance is growing alarmingly. Perhaps in time this will at least serve to give girls better standing in the marriage market. But at what a horrifying cost!

If even a fraction of this anti-women attitude had scarred the feelings of this woman who approached Jesus for healing, no wonder she is hesitant, lacking in self-esteem, wanting to stay at the edge of things, hoping just to be able to touch the edge of his cloak. Even in the telling of this story, we find Mark sandwiching the incident in as Jesus is on the way to the Synagogue official's house. It happens

"HEAVEN'S TIDE"

almost incidentally, as though the story hardly merits telling in its own right. And even today, we perform gospel-musicals about 'Jairus' Daughter'; there's unlikely to be one about 'The Woman Suffering from Chronic Haemorrhage'.

III

And so we move on to the actual *healing*. What happens when this woman and Jesus meet? Several points challenge us in the story. In the *first* place, it challenges any *simplistic view* of healing. There was no problem with the simple nature of her faith. 'If I can only touch the edge of his cloak, that will be enough.' Jesus does not ridicule this as sheer superstition as many of us probably would; as though all she wants is a magic touch. He sees it as the starting point for very real faith, as we shall see in a moment.

Yet, it is as though he is not willing to let the woman think of what she has received as merely the cure for her bleeding. 'Your faith has given you *wholeness*', he says; 'Go in *shalom*, and be *healed* of your complaint'.

In 'Heaven's Tide' the healing Bird, whose wings the woman tries to touch, takes the form of the ancient three-fold sound, AUM. Among the many meanings AUM is given in Indian tradition, the three-fold being of God is one, God who is the 'I AM' that the very name 'Ham-sa' points to. We can, then, see the Bird who flies swiftly to the help of the woman - herself a seed in the dark earth, or even a frail craft on a stormy sea - as the Triune God who from eternity seeks to bring Shalom, the fulness of peace and life, to earth and to her children.

I've used the original Hebrew term for 'peace' here, because this beautiful word evokes a wholeness and fullness of life that our word 'peace' never will. For lying behind 'shalom' is a vision of the togetherness of life, its interlocking character, that we, in our modern fragmented state, have largely lost sight of.

Well, perhaps not entirely. For recent years have seen a resurgence of that more primal, God-given sense of the way we interlock with all life: ecologically — we are bound together with all biological life in one integrated eco-system; corporately — our embodiedness means that each part of our body relates to its other parts, to our whole being as persons, and these bodies all relate to the wider body that is our God-given habitat, the body of earth as well as the social body of which we are essentially part. In this new way of seeing things, the old word *shalom* that Jesus promised this woman can now be used with so much richer meaning.

This woman, with her simple faith in the healing power of Jesus, was not to be satisfied just with a quick cure that would staunch the bleeding. She must go on to live out the wider implications of this healing, its *shalomic* wholeness of life. Neither should *we* continue to think of healing in the simplistic way we usually do. We should expect healing to go on to touch every part of our being, so that our life itself becomes a healing way.

Secondly, this story challenges any *impersonal view* of healing. Jesus was not willing to allow this woman to remain incognito, unknown to him, however shy her nature, however great the shame she felt about her condition, however 'full of fear' she was in his presence. He needed to engage in conversation with her; find out *who* it was had touched him; he wanted to know her story, and to hear it face to face. Jesus expected a *personal* engagement with this woman.

Healing can never be a merely impersonal process. The curing of a particular symptom can be, of course. Indeed, very dramatic cures can take place merely by judicious pill-popping. But one serious flaw in the practice of modern allopathic medicine is the way in which few doctors either have no time, or have no inclination to spend longer with their patients, finding out what really lies behind the obvious symptoms of which the patient first speaks. The impersonal professionalism that many doctors cultivate is often a hindrance to the healing the patient really needs.

For the human person is a wonderful blend of body, mind and spirit. From one point of view we are indeed all *body.* There is no part of our being that is not body-related, especially if we take our embodied state to mean our inter-relatedness — the air we breathe,

the water we drink, the earth that grows our food, the emotions we feel in relating to others, the deep fears we have because of hidden childhood traumas. To heal this complex kind of being that is the human person, any simplistic view of the process is doomed to be very partial, very short-term, and in the end a failure.

And there is an added dimension in the meeting of Jesus with this woman. She was in the presence of that Person who could lead her to the *shalom* God intended for her. So the shyness and diffidence compelling her to remain unnoticed, a non-person, just one of the crowd, somehow had to be overcome. Direct encounter between this Person and her innermost self, with its secrets and its suffering, its low sense of self-esteem and its unquenched hope of healing — such very personal engagement was needed if her healing was to be complete. And this engagement of the inner person, at a deeply personal level, is a key factor in the distinctiveness of the Christian view of healing — however much we Christians must be willing to learn from the New Age and the Eco-feminist movements.

When Jesus asked, 'Who touched me?', the woman, 'realising what had happened within her, and trembling with fear, knelt at his feet, telling him the whole truth'. This experience of 'fear and trembling' in the Bible is almost always when a person senses the presence of God. It was not only the healing power of Jesus, it was the very presence of Jesus that gave this woman the sense she was somehow in touch with God. And so she had to come before him, and 'tell him the whole truth'. She finds she *is* able to speak freely to him of her condition, of her-*self*; she is able to confide her secret life-story to him; she is able to speak the 'whole *truth*.' This is the kind of personal encounter between the depths of our being, our selfhood, with all its pain and its hidden secrets, and the healing selfhood of Jesus that the Gospel story invites.

IV

And, *finally*, this story challenges any false view we might have of the *cost* of healing. As medical practice becomes more and more expensive, and as more and more people are kept alive into advanced old age, one of the great questions of many societies today is — How shall we pay for it all? Who is to pay? And so every facet of medical and hospital work is 'costed'; and decisions concerning what is to be done, and who is to be treated, depend on the cost concerned. Medicine too — after many years, in Britain at least, of regarding it as a *socially shared burden* — is seen now as a matter of that ultimate Power, market forces. How long in Britain before all medical practice will be as privatised as any other public utility — water, electricity, gas, tele-communications, railways, and suchlike — that have been made private concerns recently as a result of faith in the pressure of profit as the only way people will work well?

The cost — if the healing of our life is to take place: in our personal life, our family life, our social life, our earth-life — the real cost draws in many more and wider forces than that merely of the market-place. Of the wide-ranging ways in which we will need to pay if our body is to be healed, a word from this story provides one clue. 'Jesus knew that power had gone out from him'. This was why he then asked, 'Who touched my cloak?', to the bewilderment of his disciples, when it seemed to them that in such a crowd anyone could have touched him. This sense of his loss of inner resources is in fact of a piece with the self-giving, the out-going way of Jesus in his whole ministry. It is of a piece, ultimately, with his self-giving, his out-pouring, on the cross.

All healers, in the end, are called to expend themselves in some way. Perhaps in obvious ways, as with the exhausting, caring, sometimes tedious dedication demanded of nursing. Doctors who are prepared to give more time and effort to their patients have to pay a price for their extra concern, as they seek to share their hard-won expertise with others. 'Power' goes out of them, in a way that is not true of their more easy-going colleagues. And something similar is true of priests, ministers, counsellors; why else are there so many 'broken carers' and 'wounded healers'? Even friendship has to pay a price if it's worth anything at times of crisis, when the friend is asked for a listening ear, or a comforting shoulder to cry on. It's costly, being a healing friend.

But we can extend this principle much wider than this. The healing we need for our society, for our body politic, for the earth — our mother-body — calls for, and will go on demanding from us, a costly process of giving up many of those areas of power we have acquired for ourselves. We will not be healed, will not take our part in the healing process, unless we are willing to let go of the power-systems we have come to see as our right, as necessary to our being. Here again Jesus shows us the way to our healing, to our peace. 'He knew that power had gone out of him.' And was very happy to find the woman who had been seeking healing through that power. And so she moved from suffering greatly at the edge, to that wholeness of being that it was his to give.

8 The Blind Beggar of Jericho

They came to Jericho. As Jesus and his disciples and a large crowd were leaving Jericho, Bartimaeus (meaning son of Timaeus), a blind beggar, was sitting by the roadside. When he heard that Jesus of Nazareth was passing by, he began to shout out and say, 'Jesus, Son of David, have mercy on me!' Many people sternly ordered him to be quiet, but he cried out even more loudly, 'Son of David, have mercy on me!' Jesus stood still and said, 'Call him here.' And they called the blind man, saying to him, 'Take heart; get up, he is calling you.' So throwing off his cloak, he sprang up and came to Jesus. Then Jesus said to him, 'What do you want me to do for you?' The blind man said to him, 'Rabboni, my teacher, let me see again.' Jesus said to him, 'Go; your faith has made you well.' Immediately he regained his sight and followed Jesus on the way (Mark 10:46-52).

'Let Me See Again'

He turned.
His call and look and hands
Outstretched
And waited as the blind man ran;
Not a job to be done
Not a case to be seen
Not a point to be proved
Not even a chance to reveal.
He looked with quickened tenderness
And marvelled at the blind man's
Haste.

There's an unlikely hero in our story today. But that's what most Bible characters are like: not especially gifted; few outstanding qualities; even if they were people who wielded power, few were people of great moral stature or spiritual strength. And yet, they were often the kind of characters God could do something with.

I

The *first* thing we're told about blind Bartimaeus of Jericho is that he was 'sitting by the roadside', begging for small change from the pilgrims as they passed by on their way to Jerusalem. So, as for not being an 'outstanding' person, this blind beggar was not even ordinary. His standing in society was even less than ordinary.

People had not bothered even to give him his own name. He'd been given no identity as a person in his own right. He was known only as 'son-of-Timaeus, Bar-Timaeus'. A nobody; or at least no one in particular; just a blind beggar. Most people probably walked right past him without even seeing him. He was the blind one; but they were probably less aware of him than he of them. No one would have bothered to describe things to him. Why bother with a blind beggar? But like most blind people, he would have noticed much that others missed.

This son-of-Timaeus, then, was one of those who just sat on the roadside of life; on the margin of things. Listening to the world go by. If he was born blind, he would have had little idea of what the world was like in the eyes of those with sight. But more probably he'd become blind later (for his request to Jesus was 'to see again'). So he knew what he was missing: not being able to see children's faces; not being able to see the sunlight on the river Jordan as it flowed away southwards; not being able to see the way up through the hills to God's holy city; not being able to see where he was going; not being able to work to support himself, and perhaps a family; being forced to beg for a living. For there was no welfare state, no institutes for the blind, no training programmes to help them stand on their own feet.

This son-of-Timaeus, then, was forced into 'sitting by the roadside', begging for help, just hoping for an odd pence thrown into his stretched-out hand or laid-out bit of cloth; or maybe for a scrap of food or worn-out piece of clothing; just waiting day after day for the world to pass him by. For he had no place in the mainstream of life. No place in so many of those varied activities that enrich life: reading, travelling, shopping, playing, crafts, technical skills, working at a job worth doing.

And this 'sitting by the roadside of life' is a parable of the experience of millions in the world today. The huge numbers of refugees in Africa and Asia; tribal people displaced from their forests and homelands — throughout the Americas, for example; the culturally dislocated Aboriginal people of Australia; the Dalits, the 'Broken Ones' of India; the immigrant communities of Europe; in Britain the unemployed, the homeless, the elderly on pitiful pensions. All people who have been marginalised on the roadside of the world's life. People given no standing in the world's commerce, or policy-making, or cultural main-stream. They have no power in the global market-place, no share in our affluence. Their voice is not heard by those who leave them 'sitting by the roadside'.

II

Then we come to the *second* stage of the story of this blind son-of-Timaeus. He was just not prepared to remain unnoticed and ignored. *He would not keep silent.* In all probability he spent much of each day calling out to passers-by, making his presence felt in some way. Perhaps by singing; and I've so often given money to people in India who were begging just because their singing was so beautiful; or in Britain because their musical busking on some dreary Underground station has helped to lift my travel-weary spirits.

But this son-of-Timaeus was not just doing his usual begging routine here. 'He began to *shout out*', shouting for attention, shouting to be noticed, shouting for something to be done. 'I'm here, Lord. I'm just a blind beggar. I might have no name of my own. I might have no standing in the world. But, I'm here. I'm one of the world's cast-offs that hasn't given up all hope.' And when they all told him to shut up, 'he shouted even more loudly'. He refused to be silenced.

If only those who have been pushed to the margins can be persuaded to shout about their condition, and shout even louder when the first attempts to silence them are made. Then at least there is the chance that others may join their voices with them, others whose voice carries more weight, who have more influence in places of power.

In fact, is not this task of seeking out the voiceless, the vulnerable, the marginalised, the cast-offs of our society — is not this the task of any follower of Jesus; then ensuring that they do have a voice, that they do not remain unnoticed at the roadside of life? Is not this the direct meaning of the crucial teaching passage just before this story in Mark's Gospel? Jesus has just told his followers very solemnly that to be 'great' in following him, like him they too must become 'the servant of the rest'. Or to serve 'the least of my brothers', the hungry, the naked, the needy, the oppressed. Or to open the eyes of the blind, to make the deaf to hear, to help the lame to walk, to set prisoners free, as Jesus puts in in other places.

And what was the special reason for this son-of-Timaeus to begin shouting, to demand that he be noticed? It was because he had heard that 'Jesus of Nazareth — the Healer, the Preacher of God's inbreaking reign, the One who's giving hope to the outcastes and forgotten people in the land — this Jesus is passing by right here.' There seems little doubt that he'd heard rumours before this of what Jesus had been doing. And what he heard had kindled a flame of hope. 'Why should this not be my time too? Why should I remain at the margins of life? Why should I too not share in the new things God is doing in our time, through this Jesus of Nazareth?'

So he shouted, and would not be silenced even when threatened by those around him. 'Jesus, Son of David, have pity on me.'

III

This takes us to the *third* crucial stage in the story: *'Jesus stopped and said, 'Call him'*. Here, of course, is the turning point in the story, the turning point in the life of this son-of-Timaeus. Everyone else was trying to shut him up, irritated by the disturbance he was making. 'Stop making a nuisance of yourself, you worthless piece of rubbish. It's not *your* voice we want to hear. We want to hear what this Rabbi from Galilee has to say. If we can hear him at all, perhaps he'll give us a word of blessing for the pilgrimage up to Jerusalem. We want to hear that God's kingdom is to become *ours*'.

But *Jesus heard* this voice calling out to him in desperation. Among a great clamour of voices, Jesus heard this lone voice of pleading. And he stopped to respond, to hear what lay behind this desperate cry. He had that kind of compassion that can listen, in the middle of a crowd, to the voice of what others see as a worthless beggar. 'Call him'.

And whenever, through human history, Jesus has been preached, there have been those who have experienced something similar: the certainty that he has heard their cry for help, that he has singled them out from the crowd, that his presence has in some way 'stopped' before them in his 'passing' close by, that they have received his very distinct *call* to come to him, to be with him on the road - the road of discipleship in all the ensuing events of life. One of many such, a simple evangelical song expresses the longing for such a direct call from Jesus:

Saviour, Saviour, hear my humble cry;
And while others thou art calling,
Do not pass me by.

Many more such songs — hundreds of the vast number that poured out of Charles Wesley for example — do not merely plead for such experience; they are full of the confidence that the Saviour has already called them into daily friendship with him as they face life's struggles. Hundreds, too, of the songs of faith in the indigenous styles of believers in Jesus in India are full of this same confidence. One of the few translated into English — Narayan Tilak's 'One who is all unfit to count as scholar in thy school', is just such a lyric. It goes on: 'Thou of thy love has named a friend, O kindness wonderful'. And the second stanza is equally typical of countless Indian love-faith lyrics (especially in its reference to the dust on the feet of Jesus, showing a far more authentic Galilean feel than many western hymns):

So weak am I, O gracious Lord,
So all unworthy thee,
That e'en the dust upon thy feet
Outweighs me utterly.

But equally true of the faith-experience of communities where the followers of Jesus have been a cruelly oppressed people, living at the margins of social life, has been the sense of being raised up, given a new future — *as a whole community, corporately, inclusively, and not just as scattered individuals*. In fact, the faith of a person can never be a privatised affair. In some way or another it will always mean relating to others; it will always have its community dimension.

IV

And so we are led to the *fourth* key point to note in this story - it also links with what we've been reflecting on in the above sections: the name this blind beggar uses for Jesus is very special. For the first time in Mark's Gospel Jesus is openly, publicly called 'Son of David': '*Son of David, have pity on me*'; and it's as Jesus is on his way up to the Holy City, where he has already stated emphatically, he is to be rejected and suffer and die.

The 'Son of David' can only be God's agent sent to bring in the new reign of God on earth. And the sure signs of this promised messianic age are that the lame will walk, the deaf will hear, the oppressed will be set free, *and the blind will be able to see*. The messianic age is to be an age of freedom, of wholeness, of new life, a restored world. 'Messiah', or 'Christ', means 'the Anointed One'. The image is that of one with sacred set-aside status as God's special agent. But anointing is also a sacramental sign of healing. Anointing with oil has been a common way of healing in the history of the church, as in other cultures too.

God's Anointed One, the Son of David, then, was to be a great healer. And the son-of-Timaeus uses this name to call out to Jesus. This, then, is one reason why Jesus took special notice of his shouting. He was giving voice to an insight that few others had. But such messianic hopes are always *dangerous*. They were certainly dangerous for Jesus: they were an important part in the evidence brought forward to convict him to death by the Roman occupying forces.

And they were 'dangerous' for his people to entertain; for messianic hopes can be hopelessly misleading. As Jesus was well aware. They can fill people with wild utopian dreams that have little hope of ever being fulfilled. The world God has given us is not the sort of place where absolute justice, peace, freedom, and plenty for all, can be attained by an overnight revolution, or can even be handed to us as it were on a silver platter by a divine messenger; even by this Son of David, Jesus of Nazareth.

Even in our own time we have to be aware of the dangers of messianic fantasy: a messianic mind-set inflating the role of the Christian community, as though it is inevitable that we can be God's agent for fantastic change, as though such changes do not involve a long, long process of struggle, and setback, and disappointment, and rethinking, and re-struggling. It was just this kind of messianic fantasy that Jesus turned his back on, at whatever cost, when he was tempted at the time of being anointed in baptism, anointed for this messianic role.

If we are to follow Jesus, Christians must never allow themselves to become messianic fantasists, any more than messianic fanatics. And they must certainly never be seduced into thinking that any particular political programme or party, however sincerely committed to social justice, will inevitably bring in God's new world. Following Jesus means going on carrying his cross, sharing his ignominy and failure; and such cross-sharing will continue to be an essential part even of messianic faith.

Did our blind beggar perhaps have just this insight? We do not know for certain. But we do know that for Jesus too this man's acclamation of faith was crucial. The new sight he received from the hand of Jesus was itself a sign of the inner sight, the illumining, that was this blind man's. For this last healing story in Mark comes at a crucial moment; and most of the story is about this otherwise unknown blind beggar, rather than about what *Jesus* did. The son-of-Timaeus had become a powerful sign in the retelling of the

"AMAZING LOVE"

Jesus story; a sign of what true messianic faith in Jesus can be.

The way by which the blind man sits here in Jyoti's 'Amazing Love' is a bewildering, mystifying maze. And yet Jesus himself is that Way, in which there are many different phases and many different layers of meaning. It is a Way on which the disciple sets out in faith, trusting that further insight into the meaning of this Way will be disclosed as the journey with Jesus unfolds.

As soon as the people around him stop their insults and chiding, as soon as he hears that Jesus was calling him, the blind man knew the great moment to change his life had come. We're told that first he 'threw off his cloak'. This sign of his beggarliness, of his worthlessness, of his sitting around by the roadside asking for handouts; this was thrown off. Then we are told that he 'sprang to his feet, and came forward to Jesus', to meet the one he'd openly called 'Son of David'.

'What is it you want me to do for you', Jesus asks. Obviously he can see the man is blind. But he needs to hear his request for healing; in effect, it would be a further public expression of his faith, his faith not just that Jesus has healing power. There is more than that. There is faith that, as they set off for the final confrontation with those who opposed this new way, *Jesus is able to provide a clear sign of the inbreaking of God's power to change things.* 'Rabbuni', the blind beggar replies, 'I want my sight again'. This request to 'see', of course, refers to his inner vision, his ability to see the meaning of all that Jesus is doing, and all that he is to go through at Jerusalem, as well as to the physical eyesight that he's lost. So the title, 'My Rabbi', usually translated 'Master', is very close in meaning to 'My Guru': for he sees Jesus as a teacher that can lead him 'from darkness into light'. But, we'll look at this illumining role of Jesus — in giving sight to the blind — when we reflect on John's story of a blind man.

'Go, your faith has made you whole', was Jesus' response to the blind beggar's request. So it was far more than just the recovery of his sight. It is 'wholeness' that he is to receive, the completeness of being that is God's purpose for his children. This is, of course, very different from the kind of super-beings that glossy magazines, as well as scientologists and various kinds of spiritualities of our time, urge us to try to become. There we are urged to expect a physical perfection in which there seems no room for any weakness or flaw. We are to attain unlimited mental powers. We are to be ever-successful in social skills. We are to achieve phenomenal soul-growth that makes even the Creator seem a spiritual pygmy. We are to possess transcendent soul-force able to throw off all our social and historical conditioning. This is not the 'wholeness' Jesus promises. For the son-of-Timaeus it was, rather, to be a new life free from the demeaning, marginalising beggarliness of his past. He now no longer sits at the roadside, but goes off as one of those following Jesus, even if his discipleship has to be worked out painfully on the road following Jesus to his place of self-sacrifice. This is no cheap and easy wholeness of life. But it is, nevertheless, a promise that even this previously blind beggar was to be part of the fullness of God's purpose in creation, the promise that even he would share in all the blessings intended by God in bringing his and all life into being. Healing is to lead on to the wholeness of being that is God's creative purpose for all his creatures.

9 The Hidden Healer & the Alien Woman

Jesus set out and went away to the region of Tyre. He entered a house and did not want anyone to know he was there. But he could not be hidden. A woman whose little daughter had an unclean spirit immediately heard about him, and she came and bowed down at his feet. Now the woman was a Gentile, of Syro-phoenecian origin. She begged him to cast the demon out of her daughter. Jesus said to her, 'Let the children be fed first, for it is not fair to take the children's food and throw it to the dogs.' But she answered him, 'Sir, even the dogs under the table eat the children's crumbs.' Then he said to her, 'For saying that, you may go - the demon has left your daughter.' She went home, found the child lying on the bed, and the demon gone (Mark 7:24-30 and Matthew 15:21-28).

'He Could Not be Hidden'

He could not be hidden
In the outhouse of an inn,
Nor in small-town, down-town Nazareth
Nor in the bosom of his family.
He could not escape from the crowd
To the singing hills, and waters of Galilee.
His secrets became the rage of the town,
He could not perform, or conform
To the wail or the pipings of
The petulant children of Israel.
He could not pass unnoticed
In upmarket holy Jerusalem
But caused a furore midst
The cages and tables and changers.
He would not be nailed down,
Bouldered in;
But quietly, for ever, stepped over the rim
And now our hidden longings
Are starlit, but secret in Him.

Many of the healing stories of Jesus have some strange features. There's Mad Mob of the Gadarene Caves; there's the Astonishing Faith of an Enemy; there's the Woman at the Edge of Things; there's the Wailing for a Sleeping Child (all of which we'll come to later). And there are many more. This *strangeness* of the way Jesus was and the way he acts is a strong part of his appeal. It was even then, and tells us why people 'were filled with wonder' and 'awe' when they saw him in action. So our own sense of the oddity of some aspects of these healings of Jesus are not just because it all happened in an alien culture far away and long ago. That too — their rootedness in a real and peculiar history — is part of the power of these stories. There's nothing invented or contrived or artificial about them.

I've called her just 'The Alien Woman', though the Gospel story of her says she was 'Syro-Phoenician'. 'Canaanite' would be a simpler term, indicating clearly enough her alien status as far as Jewish people were concerned. Her's is a story that has as many oddities — bits that need special explanation for us — as any of Jesus' healings.

I

First, we begin with the devil. It wasn't the woman who had 'an evil spirit', but her daughter. The mother had come pleading for the daughter she loved. She was distraught in the belief that her daughter was devil-possessed. And she was desperate in her desire that this evil spirit be exorcised. Their's was a culture, as was Jesus' own, that found evil spirits at work in all manner of sickness, physical as well as mental, and at work in animals, trees, crops, springs; in fact at work anywhere in creation where things seem to be going wrong. Rural life in India and indeed all over the world finds such evil spirits at work when things go against us.

Jesus accepted this same view of the demonic, and worked within just such a world. It is not only his radical criticism of accepted attitudes, but his cultural rootedness too, that make up the strength of the Jesus story. He works within the real world of his people's experience, within their perceptual conditioning. Jesus meets people just where they are.

But if that's not where *we* are, what are we to make of it? There are, of course, many people even in urbanised society today who are quite prepared to accept this same view of lurking demons. For some, their reasoning is, if it was Jesus' way of seeing things, it's not only good enough for me; it's a worldview all must hold.

That there *is* evil in the world; that there *are* things that have gone wrong in God's creation; that *conflict* is inescapable if we are to be agents of the new world God has promised; that this conflict will often be with structured, focused evil, so that it will seem like a struggle with *demonic powers* — all this is undeniable. In some cultures the power of conviction is such that only the exorcising of what is seen as an evil spirit within will effect a cure. Sometimes, indeed, we might well feel that *accounting for* the evil that blights the life of our world in terms of demonic powers is the only option. Or is at least as good an option as any other for this mystery of evil. How else can we account for God's good creation going so terribly and painfully wrong at so many points? But we need to be very clear about the dangers of demon-talk — in the horrifying way mental illness was treated in the past, for example.

And are we also clear about what, according to Christian faith, God has already done in the conflict with evil? This is a power that has already lost its potency to do any decisive damage to us. These evil forces have no lasting place in God's creation. The decisive battle against them is already over - according to New Testament faith. We have been set free from the grip of any such powers (Cols 2:15). No longer can they distress, torment, destroy the life God gives us.

But this woman from Canaan, alien even to the Jewish world of Jesus, let alone the world of apostolic faith, was hardly able to share this kind of belief. Her plea is very simple, as she 'fell at his feet': 'Drive out my daughter's demon.'

II

And there is a *second* odd feature found at the beginning of this story. It begins with Jesus the Healer trying to remain hidden. No doubt this was the very reason for his journey to alien country. This was a stage in his ministry when he needed to be alone with his close circle of friends, undisturbed by the thronging crowds, many clamouring for his healing touch.

But the story tells us: 'He could not stay hidden.' How often in ancient Indian stories of God's playfulness with his lovers, those aflame with passionate longing for his presence, God hides himself. And his loved ones are beside themselves, inconsolably desolate with the pain of separation. Eventually, of course, God always comes to his loved ones again, and there is the bliss of re-union.

Why, though, think only of the dramatic stories of the mythic past of India? There is the experience of Methodist God-lovers of earlier generations in my own tradition. Almost all went through periods of grieving for their loss of any sense of God's presence. God was, for a time that seemed like an eternity, hidden from them. And even for those who lack this kind of passion in their faith, much of the time God's presence is far from obvious. A *deus absconditus,* a 'God who hides himself', is for many people of faith, for much of the time, the only God they know. And this is God's way with his creation. God never forces faith, or it would not be faith. God's presence is always wrapped in mystery.

No more could Jesus accept the demand some made at times in his ministry for 'signs' beyond all refuting. Was not every public act of his a sufficiently potent and authentic sign that God was now present in a new way, at work in a new way? To demand proof beyond this was to put God to trial; it was a denial of the way of faith.

So Jesus, here in this distant place of attempted hiding, was in tune with God's ways. No doubt his concern was also to spend time with his closest followers, further guiding them into God's secret, yet open ways. It was not the right time for public acts of healing. But, as the Gospel puts it: 'He could not stay hidden.' Even when he did not seek confrontation with the forces of evil in God's world, he is discovered. There was no hiding his healing presence; at least for those who have faith.

That the wings of the Bird are like the rays of the sun is brought out vividly in this Jyoti's 'Hidden Healing'. And how can the Sun finally be hidden? The rays of healing light burst from the Bird's heart; and the woman, though an 'alien', is enthralled. In spite

"HIDDEN HEALING"

of the challenging, almost threatening aura of the Sun-Bird's presence, the woman calls out in faith, and Love does its healing work in her child - the demon is exorcised.

III

And this brings us to the *third* odd feature of the story: the person who discovers the hidden healer. For a start she is a *woman*, a lower order creature according to many societies as well as the Jewish society of which Jesus was part. The blatant sexual exploitation of women in modern western culture, the burning of women because of less dowry than demanded, the refusal by some Islamic zealots to allow women any public role, the female infanticide of China, the circumcising of women in parts of Africa — these and many more oppressive, often violent acts against women are all of a piece with the demeaning of women in the society of Jesus' time.

And Jesus openly many times, implicitly always, rejected this demeaning of women. True, women were not included in the inner circle of those chosen to share his mission. Here the culture of his time dictated the apostolic gender. But just recall: his compassion for the widow of Nain; his conversing with the woman at the Samaritan well; his uncondemning treatment of the woman caught in adultery; his joy in the extravagant devotion of a prostitute; his close understanding with and clear respect for Mary at Bethany; the fact that women were those who stood closest to his cross, and were first to witness to his rising again. Are these not convincing proof of the new freedom that Jesus expected for women? He gave them a new standing.

And this woman was also an 'alien', a foreign Gentile, a Syrian, not one of the chosen community. True, she 'fell at his feet'. But in the eyes probably even of Jesus' disciples, she had no right at all to speak to their Jewish Rabbi. She certainly had no right to ask him a favour, such as the healing of her daughter. Yet this is what she does. Jesus does not seem to respond immediately to her plea. But we come to that in a moment. In the end, her courage, her temerity, her tenacity on her daughter's behalf delighted Jesus. She just would not be silent; she would not give up in the face of what at first seems indifference. And Jesus was delighted. So this was the person who discovered the Hidden Healer in their midst; and she was rewarded.

IV

There is a *fourth* feature of this story that calls for explanation. What are we to make of the response that Jesus first makes to this woman? 'Let us first feed the children. It is not right to take the children's food and throw it to the dogs'? Gentiles, those not of the chosen people of God, were sometimes known as 'dogs'. Such was the disdain for those outside the pale felt by many Jews of the time. And theirs is not the only religious or ethnic community to feel nothing but disgust towards people of other communities. It is the basis of the dreadful 'ethnic cleansing' that has resulted in such cruel consequences in Bosnia. For people of Christian communities to be perpetrating such inhuman crimes against Muslims, whatever their histories might have been, is a blasphemous rejection of the way of Jesus. There are so many decisive pointers in Jesus' teaching, as in his actions towards those who were not Jews, to make it abundantly clear that Jesus urges us never to confront others merely on the basis of their religious allegiance, or their ethnic origin. But we will take this up in another context. Here in this story, then, why does Jesus speak of 'dogs'? To me it seems clear that Jesus was at first quoting a common proverb to this 'alien woman'. Perhaps there is also a moment of testing; assessing her sincerity.

Gurus in India quite normally begin with some word of discouragement, in their initial response to an enquirer. It could be that Jesus too is just probing to find out of what sort her faith really is: 'Look, this is what my folk say about your folk - that you have no right at all to be asking for "bread" that is intended for the chosen children. What do you make of that?'

Her response delights him. 'Even the dogs under the table eat the children's left-overs.' In response to such a buoyant spirit, there was no way that Jesus would not have given her what she asked. One wonders, in fact, if there was not a lively chuckle along with his acceptance of her plea. In any case her answer delighted him, and his own response was immediate: 'Because of that answer, go back home; you will find that the demon has gone out of your daughter.' And it had. The mother found her 'lying on her bed', i.e. she was now restful, in her right mind, at ease again, untroubled by whatever had been tormenting her. 'Alien' though this woman's faith was probably in so many respects, she was one of the few able to see into the heart of Jesus. She had discovered the hidden healer in their midst. Now she seemed to know that his first word, however discouraging on the surface, was not the last word he had to say to her. She had that insight into the mind of Jesus that prompted her to persevere. She seemed to know of what sort his compassion really was. And her own heart's desire was granted. Crumbs from the table, children's left-overs or not, her little girl was healed.

10 Ephphatha: Open Up

Then Jesus returned from the region of Tyre, and went by way of Sidon towards the Sea of Galilee, in the region of the Ten Towns. They brought to him a deaf man who had an impediment in his speech; and they begged him to place his hand upon him. Jesus took him aside in private, away from the crowd, and put his fingers into his ears, and spat and touched his tongue. Then looking up to heaven, he sighed and said to him, 'Ephphatha', that is, 'Be opened.' And immediately his ears were opened, his tongue was set free, and he spoke plainly. Then Jesus ordered them to tell no one; but the more he ordered them, the more zealously they proclaimed it. They were astonished beyond measure, saying, 'He has done everything well; he even makes the deaf to hear and the mute to speak.' (Mark 7:31-37).

The Wonder of Sound

His ears and heart opened
And the dawn streamed in.
He heard with the ears
Of one straining to waken.
He listened and savoured
As one for the first or last time
Hearing the breath of the spirit
Breathing out in the wind,
Nodding and meeting
Light through the leaves,
The stealth of a whisper
Blown up to a breeze,
The fall of a laugh
The climb of a moan
The burst of a pod
And the scrape on the ground.
Each came alive and aloud,
For the world was lit up
With the wonder of sound.

Our story today is that of Jesus healing a 'deaf-mute'. I'm sure this is another case where we should be using some other term for this disability. No doubt there's a long list of more 'correct' terms with which we can raise a bit of a laugh. 'Vocally and auditively challenged' — ludicrous new nomenclature of that sort, intended of course to lessen the sense of stigma that deaf-mutes carry with them. For, let's make no mistake, deaf-mutes suffer stigma, as well as a sense of estrangement. I saw again just recently the wonderfully sensitive film of that classic novel about a deaf-mute, *The Heart is a Lonely Hunter.* A very moving piece of drama.

And I remembered clearly the pang of fear I felt as a child when a deaf-mute came into our house. My father was a farmer in rural North Devon, and needed a farmhand. George C. from the village asked if we would not consider his brother, and he brought him over for an interview. The brother had no hearing, and therefore could not speak normally. In fact he frequently broke into a stream of unearthly wild-sounding noises. Then there were also his outbursts of violent anger, no doubt due to his frustration with the hand he'd been dealt in life. To the children of our village, including us, he seemed to be a madman either to be dreaded, or cruelly mimicked. My father was outstandingly just and kind-hearted; but he did not feel able to employ this man. There seemed to be too many problems.

A deaf-mute is not just a person with hearing and therefore speaking difficulties. And yet, few people hold the same sympathy for a deaf-mute that they will feel for, let's say, a person with blindness, or paralysis, or even epilepsy. But of all the people Jesus healed, this deaf-mute probably suffered as much as any.

I

We note *first* the region in which this took place. Mark's geography is not entirely clear, but at this point in his Gospel several incidents are located in areas *outside* of Jewish homeland. They follow Jesus' teaching about purity and impurity not being a matter of ritual observance; what is important is the heart being faithful to God. It is *not* a question of belonging to the right ethnic group. Then there is the story of the Syrian mother pleading for her daughter's healing, and by her faith and wit receiving some 'bread from the children's table'.

And this little collection of events outside the holy land closes with a second miraculous feeding in a desert place — this time of 4000 people, with seven loaves of bread, and ending with seven baskets full of the leftovers. All no doubt intended as signs of the fullness of the messianic feast for the fullness of the Gentile people. I can hardly help but recall the ancient Vedic word concerning the mystery of creation: 'From the fulness comes this fulness, yet fulness remains.'

So this deaf-mute is a man of Decapolis, the Ten Towns not far from Galilee that had been deliberately populated with non-Jewish people. It was part of an earlier Hellenising programme; and it created a potential meeting-point of Jew and Greek. Was not Mark's intention in putting in this brief batch of stories from outside the old boundaries to show that the words and acts of Jesus are quite able to arouse faith in people there too? His healing work is effective for *all*; those belonging to other ethnic and religious communities are in no way *outsiders* to this new movement that is taking place through Jesus. For anyone, anywhere, is within the compass of God's renewing grace. No one is an 'outsider' to God. Why, then, are some features of this story so very Jewish — the key-word, the Aramaic '*ephphatha*' for one ? And why do people see clues to Jesus' messianic character, and witness to this openly, if they are not the people expecting the Messiah? Is not this the Gospel's way of saying that 'outsiders' too are both touched by this Messiah's ministry, and are able to be witness to his special role in God's purpose?

And missionary movements ever since confirm this, in spite of the unbelievably crass insensitivity of so many missionaries to the cultural context in which they have served. The responses of people in amazingly diverse lands have shown just how strangely potent the words and acts of Jesus are in evoking similar kinds of response to that of people in the Gospel story. Age-old expectations are strangely fulfilled. For this 'messianic' work of his — especially his healing work in the wide range of its meaning is essentially about renewing our *humanness*, restoring us to a God who is passionately concerned about our humanness, as the late Dr. M.M.Thomas (who sadly died just a few days ago) put it in the title of one of his books, *Salvation is Humanization.* And to this humans everywhere can bear witness. How few missionaries, however, have actively encouraged the diversity of life-style and faith-expression that a 'humanising' gospel evokes! For in their humanness, people have such very distinctive histories and expectations and ways of looking at the world, and therefore very different ways of responding to Jesus. Unless, that is, that 'response' is so controlled by culture-bound missionary tradition that little in the response is truly *in-born, indi-genous.* The more fully indigenous is faith in and witness to Christ in any country, the more authentic is that faith and witness; the more true it is to the messianic work of Jesus as the one who heals and restores our humanness.

II

The *second* special feature of this story is the balance of the *support of other people,* along with the *need for aloneness.* It is because 'some people' were concerned about this deaf-mute, bringing him along to Jesus and 'begging Jesus to place his hands upon him', that he found himself in this place of healing in the presence of Jesus. Most likely they were family, for it would be quite rare then for a deaf-mute to have many friends.

Several other healing stories make a similar point: parents, family, friends, supporters - so often it is their faith that Jesus commends, *their* effort that leads to healing. We all need our support-groups in some form or other, for we are creatures whose essential being is inter-dependent. The sense of *belonging* that this deaf-mute surely had, the confidence that others cared for him, was no doubt the first step towards healing.

Yet, the first thing Jesus does is to take him off 'alone, away from the crowd', away from his family. It's what he was also doing regularly with his inner group of followers: taking them off alone, away from the crowd, creating quiet space for them.

The encompassing wings of the heavenly Bird form an ear for the deaf-mute in Jyoti's 'Listening, Opening'. He struggles to hear, crouching low, rock-like, to listen to earth's sounds. Like the heavenly Swan of legend, Jesus whispers in his ears, words that reach his inmost self. The healed man is like the prophet Elijah in the cave, listening to the 'still, small voice' of God.

And that is why Jesus often spoke of the need to be willing to leave behind our families, if we're to follow him. Our concern, our commitments need to go beyond even our family loyalty, beyond any merely group faith.

While faith in what Jesus can do, faith in his healing power, can never be a *private* affair, as so many conservative believers would like us to believe, it must always be a *personal* experience, a relationship with this Man-who-leads-us-to-God which draws out from us our unique way of being a human person. Each person's very special way of being human and therefore of responding to the meaning of Jesus for us is what is to be expected. Conditioning by others — teachers, parents, friends, the cultural life that has made us what we are — all this is a very necessary part of that process of becoming human, and so of finding ourselves. There is no selfhood for us without that prior conditioning. But no one who has not gone on to distance themselves from the society that moulded them, not able in crucial ways to detach themselves from the opinions and traditions that others have devised, can claim to be fully human, or can come to see the special meaning the coming of Jesus has for them. A personal response is called for, as my Methodist forbears were adamant about in their preaching. Jesus first 'took him off alone, away from the crowd'.

III

Thirdly, the next series of actions by Jesus seem to modern readers of the story very strange indeed. He 'put his fingers in the man's ears, spat, and touched the man's tongue. Then Jesus. . . gave a deep groan, and said *ephphatha*'.

"LISTENING, OPENING"

The plea of his family, of course, had been that Jesus would 'place his hands on him'. The hand-touch of the Healer was crucial, as we have seen in so many of these stories. Here Jesus is very specific: the ears and the tongue need to be touched. But did they? In other stories we sometimes read that the *word* of Jesus was sufficient, perhaps even when the sufferer was not even present.

Here, though, there had been the family's specific request that Jesus lay his hands on this deaf-mute. Their prayer could well be taken as the prayer we all of us need to make whenever we, or anyone we love, seek healing of any kind, by any means. When we go to see a doctor, or into hospital, into the operating theatre, or when some other healer lays hands upon us — our prayer can be this same prayer: 'My Lord, lay *your* hands upon him/her/me'.

It was, then, in response to the plea of the family that Jesus laid hands on this man's ears and tongue. And it may be that the man himself needed these outward signs of re-assurance, along with the use of the healer's saliva, his groaning and looking up to heaven. For all these acts were typical of the local healers of Jesus' time. There is no reason at all not to accept gladly the fact that there were other charismatic healers, as well as the physicians of the period (of whom Luke was one, you may recall). That Jesus ministered in some ways just like others in no way diminishes the very special meaning and effect of his healing acts.

In any case, Jesus saw that *this* was the manner in which this particular person was to be healed. Probably his confidence had been severely eroded over the years. Years of ridicule, being the butt of people's mimicry and cruel joking, must have left him with a psyche sadly lacking in self-confidence. Healing is always very dependent on confidence; often the confidence created by the healer's manner and what is said and done, even if only to create the illusion that something significant has been done. What else are placebos, and how else do these harmless replacements for the real thing do their good work? If nothing else, then, this series of pre-healing acts would have re-assured the deaf-mute. But there is more than this in Jesus' actions. To use his saliva, his spittle, to anoint the man's ears and tongue was a sign that the inner life and power of Jesus, his very Spirit was now at work in this person, healing, restoring, recreating.

Yes, just as in the process of creating God had mixed earth and water, and had then breathed Spirit into this 'earth-being' to bring human life into being, so Jesus was re-creating a human person, restoring to the life intended in God's purpose. And that is what healing is all about: receiving the healing, life-giving Spirit of Jesus, so that there is a 'new creation', to use the Apostle's words.

And the *groaning* of Jesus? Well, we are told that the coming to birth of God's new creation will be like a woman going through birth-pains, before the new being finally breaks through into the world. And there was pain and struggle on Jesus' part in all this healing activity. Pain in seeing how disfigured, for whatever reason, was the good creation of God. Pain in sharing the suffering of those who flocked to him for healing. 'Compassion', suffering-with, is the term used just two verses after this story, as Jesus sees their hunger and their need. It was a heart of compassion, God's heart, that must have *always* felt some form of identifying pain. Then there was pain in the resolve and effort and struggle required to confront the various forms of evil lying behind people's suffering - both spiritual forces of evil, and the accumulating antagonism of religious authority and tradition opposing his movement for a new world. And this was an antagonism to change that in the end took him to the culminating pain of the cross. All this and more lies behind the deep-felt groaning of Jesus, as he looks to heaven, seeking the continuing help and strength of God for his work.

IV

Finally, there is the healing word, in the original Aramaic of Jesus' own language, *ephphatha*, 'open up'. Just by pronouncing this word we get some idea of the wonderfully forceful way in which it can be said. 'Ephphatha!' But its meaning is the more important point. 'Open up'. The 'opening up' of eyes, ears, mouth, of closed hearts, of imprisoned existence, of the way forward - all these acts of 'opening' were to characterise the new age of the Anointed One to come.

The deaf-mute here is a person with his own painful past from which he is to be released. But he is also a sign of people's inability and unwillingness to listen to what God is saying through Jesus and through his healing acts. He is a sign of people's failure to respond to what is happening through Jesus and *speak out clearly* about the inbreaking of God's new age. Of course many of them were impressed by the *cures* being done. But most, though not all, were missing the point, the hidden point of the healing. That's why Jesus tries to turn their minds away from the miracle as such.

'Open up', says Jesus. For it is our closed-in mentality, our being tied up within ourselves, our self-obsessed outlook, that is both the cause of our unresponsiveness to the challenge of Jesus, and the cause of much of our sickness. Turned in upon ourselves, we are unable to respond freely to the myriad blessings that God offers us in creation, often healing blessings. Instead, then, of rejoicing in the beauty and bounty of God's staggeringly wonderful world, our habitat, with our self-obsessed view of things we become a destructive curse to creation.

'Open up', says Jesus. Open your whole bodies to what God offers you in creation; open your whole selves to the healing and restoring you can receive through the work God is doing through me. Then you will be able to hear of God's goodness and love through a thousand voices each day. Then you will have the courage to speak out against all that is cruelly opposed to that way of goodness and love; speak out on behalf of those still in need of God's basic blessings, still homeless, hungry and thirsty, unable to speak for themselves; speak out for this new way of healing and restoring in God's kingdom. No wonder some said of Jesus; 'How well he does everything (as promised by God).'

11 The Healing Pool

After this there was a festival of the Jews, and Jesus went up to Jerusalem. Now in Jerusalem by the Sheep Gate there is a pool, called in Hebrew Bethesda, which has five porticoes. In these lay many invalids, blind, lame, and paralyzed. One man was there who had been ill for thirty-eight years. When Jesus saw him lying there and knew that he been there a long time, he said to him, 'Do you want to be made well?' The sick man answered him, 'Sir, I have no one to put me into the pool when the water is stirred up; and while I am making my way, someone else steps down ahead of me.' Jesus said to him, 'Stand up, take your mat and walk.'

Now that day was a sabbath. So the Jews said to the man who had been cured, 'It is the sabbath; it is not lawful for you to carry your mat.' But he answered them, 'The man who made me well said to me, "Take up your mat and walk"' They asked him, 'Who is the man who said to you, "Take it up and walk"?' Now the man who had been healed did not know who it was, for Jesus had disappeared in the crowd that was there. Later Jesus found him in the temple and said to him, 'See, you have been made well! Do not sin any more, so that nothing worse happens to you.' The man went away and told the Jews that it was Jesus who had made him well. Therefore they started persecuting Jesus, because he was doing such things on the sabbath. But Jesus answered them, 'My Father is still working, and I also am working.' For this reason the Jews were seeking all the more to kill him, because he was not only breaking the sabbath, but was also calling God his own Father, thereby making himself equal to God (John 5:1-18).

"Bathe me in the bathing of thy pool."

What irked and gnawed and ground him down
Was the scalding feeling of being ignored.
He could say "Go", and no one would go.
He could say "Come", and no one would come.
He would say "Do this" and that was not done.

He was an impotent, pent-in man
Unarmed, but with murderous intent
Left to fester with his rage unspent.
The order was given to get up and walk;
And to his surprise he did without thought,
The urge to command and demand
For a moment submerged
In a greater one's will.

Today's story is the first from John's Gospel. So far all the stories we have looked at are from one or other of the first three Gospels. The difference in John's style and mood is immediately obvious. And this makes it clear that the *teller* of these stories too is an important factor in the impact they make on us. When John tells his stories of Jesus, more than is so with the other Gospel-writers, his reflection on their meaning is already part of the stories themselves. And so at many points in the stories there is insight into their meaning already made explicit. This is just what we find in John's story (John 5:1-17, 26) of the man disabled in Bethesda.

In older translations the man is called a 'cripple'. Now an offensive term, we might note that originally it meant one who had to creep along; so this would have been an accurate literal description of this man's condition. There's even reason, as we see later in the story, for thinking of this man as 'a bit of a *creep*', for he was not a very likeable character as it turned out.

Even so, he was a person in great need, one of the disabled people gathered round that healing pool at Bethesda. Sacred power — perhaps a powerful underground spring with healing properties — was said to 'move the waters' every now and then. And if you could immerse yourself in the water immediately this divine stirring occurred, healing was assured. Or so it was claimed. And the crowds of people seeking health were there waiting for the moment of 'visitation'. Many times I have, in India, seen great crowds of people dipping themselves into the waters of pools at sacred places: perhaps a pool around which a temple is built. Perhaps a powerful spring like that which surges out miraculously each year at the sacred site of the Great Bull at Nandyal in Andhra Pradesh. Or perhaps one of the great sacred rivers. For many years I lived on the banks of the sacred river Godavari. An early morning walk would see devout women hurrying back home, clothes still dripping with water even in the cold of the few weeks of winter. And during the days of the great festival of Pushkaram, held at different sacred rivers every 14 years, several millions people from far and wide came for their holy bath. Purification was what they sought; purity of body and soul — in other words, wholeness of life here and the bliss of heaven to come. Some came with fervent prayers for healing; and no doubt some prayers were answered.

It was to one such healing pool that Jesus came, and saw the crowds seeking wholeness and healing. As usual, of course, Jesus doesn't just see a crowd. He focuses on one person, and on that person's particular need.

I

First, then, *Jesus begins with a question, a question that goes right to the heart of this man's condition.* 'Do you *want* to be healed'? Do you really *want* to be different from how you now are? Do you really *want* things to be changed? The point is, this man had a chronic problem. For 38 years he'd been in this state of immobility. And even though he was so near the healing pool, he was unable to take advantage of any 'moving of the waters'. So the question Jesus puts is this: Do you still believe that God has something new for your life? Is the flame of hope still burning in your spirit? Or, have you become so used to this static life that you've come to think that nothing can change things now?' It must have been all too easy to sink into the lethargy of despair; to feel that any further hope is useless, mere wishful thinking which just leaves you with further pain and the bitter taste of disillusionment.

If it were in India, Jesus would have asked this man: 'Are you a *mumukshu*? Are you seeking to be free, for all eternity, from the fetters of your mortality?' 'Lead me', says the ancient text of the Upanishads, 'Lead me from the unreal into reality; lead me from darkness to light; lead me from death to immortal life'. This intense search for liberation from all the bondage of our present existence was what has typified Indian spiritual longing through the ages.

There is an oft-told story of a young man coming to the feet of a Guru deep in meditation beside the waters of one of the great sacred rivers. 'Swamiji', the young seeker pleaded, 'you are the one who can lead me to inner freedom'. For a long time the holy man said nothing, stayed unmoving. Three times the young man asked, each time with more direct pleading: 'Guru, please teach me the way of liberation'. Finally the holy man seized the young man by the scruff of the neck, plunged his head into the river, and held him there until he almost drowned. When he eventually came up spluttering and asking why he'd been so roughly treated, when all he'd done was ask for guidance, the Swamiji replied: 'When you long for liberation as you just now longed for air, then perhaps there is a chance I can lead you to freedom'.

'Do you *want* to be made well?', asked Jesus. He is probably also pointing to something deeper than merely this man's will to walk, to have the strength and the functioning of his legs again. Jesus is also asking: 'Do you have that flame of desire, that inner longing, for life at a different level from that which you have been living? Do you have a real interest in that new way of living and loving, that free movement of the spirit that makes life so different? Do you want healing of that kind?'

II

Then we move on to the *second* key moment in this story. What ever failing there may have been in this crippled man's character - failings no doubt exacerbated a hundred times by the frustrations and humiliations of being known as a 'cripple' - his reply to Jesus was enough. 'I have no one to help me'. 'I have no one to lift me so that I can reach the pool of healing at that moment when there is healing power'.

How crucial is the help of others. To be human is to be dependent, dependent upon what others say and do, for good and for evil. Even those we call great individualists, the truly original and creative people in human history, have in reality been deeply conditioned by what others have said and been and done: mothers, lovers, teachers, earlier key figures in their 'world of discourse', history-makers, house-builders, gardeners, food-producers, water-engineers; and then all those upon whom these and many more are themselves dependent — the list is literally endless. The 17th century preacher, poet, lover, and Dean of St. Paul's Cathedral, John Donne, put it in this way: 'No man is an island. . .' To be human is to be dependent, through and through dependent upon what others have done, and what they now do.

Right-wing rhetoric makes much of the need to banish the 'dependency culture'. It was even notoriously claimed by Margaret Thatcher that there is no such thing as 'society', only individuals formed into temporary groups for the sake of mutual gain. To deny in this way that our human togetherness is not essential to our nature, to deny that it is only through our interacting in human communities that our individuality emerges, is to dangerously mislead.

And what are we to make of those religious faiths which claim that the liberation we should seek is one that removes altogether this natural dependence we are born with? How should we judge a religious worldview which says so that we should aim to move beyond all relational life and on to pure independent self-being? Too few Christian theologians in India have seen the significance of the great clash of worldview *within* Indian traditions. In India's religious ferment, some have dismissed all relational life as the great bondage; others have held that it is in loving relationship, especially in our dependence upon God, that our salvation lies. If it is a choice between these two, surely Christian faith can see where its options lie. We are committed to a God who has created for us, and placed us in, a world where our inter-dependence is everything. To be human in the way God wants us to be, is to be dependent upon each other. We need each other's help if we are to find God's purpose for us.

It is especially for those who are sick, those who need healing, that the help, the support, the encouragement, the touch, of others is so essential. Unlike that paralysed man who was carried to Jesus by four of his friends, this man, it seems, had no one to help him. Such aloneness, for most people, is devastating. The warm springs of our humanity become chilled. The friendless person is often an inwardly frozen person. In the case of this man at the healing pool, it's quite

"IN GATHERING"

possible that he had become crippled within, in his inner self as much as in his outer body. 'I have no one to help me.'

No wonder, then, that for Jesus this man's reply was sufficient: 'I have no one to help me'. Here was pathos at a level certain to touch the heart of one who's compassion, who's capacity to suffer with and for others, in the end took him to the cross. Along with such compassion, however, there is also complete authority in the words with which Jesus responds: 'Get up; take up your mat, and walk'.

In Jyoti's 'In-gathering' we are reminded of the tear-stressed saying of Jesus quoted in the Prologue: 'I would have gathered you under my wings like a mother-bird, but you...did not know the time of your peace'. So engrossing is the mother-bird love of Jesus for God's holy city - the 'place of God's peace' - that the heavenly Bird's wings are one with the city walls. It was outside these same walls to which he was taken for his criminal's death. Just as at the healing pool, people lay sleeping, waiting for the promised Shalom of new life.

III

And this takes us to the *third* main issue in this story: the *healing authority of Jesus.* The authority here is that of one who *knows what God's real intention for his children is, has the power to convince this man such healing is God's will for him, and thus is able to communicate the healing power of God.* Jesus seemed just to emanate this authority.

The Gospel writer has in fact taken this question of the authority of Jesus as the big issue in the story. He follows the story of the healing with the longest, most explicit affirming of Jesus' divine authority in the whole Gospel. The point at issue between Jesus and the religious authorities of his time was the fact that he had healed on the Sabbath, the day divinely set aside for rest. Any form of work not absolutely necessary for life, was taboo. Yet Jesus seems regularly to have continued his healing work on this divinely ordained rest day. Why ? - was the challenge of those whose duty it was to maintain the sanctity of this Sabbath day.

The reply of Jesus floods our minds with insight into his new way. 'My Father is always at work, and I too must work.' God is at work all the time, without rest, giving life, providing for life, restoring broken life, healing lives that are crippled for countless reasons. Every time, then, the word of a friend, or a counsellor, helps to restore confidence to a depressed person; every time a homeless child is given shelter and wholesome food; every time a nurse tends the ulcers of an elderly person; every time a doctor works for the well-being of a patient; every time a country's social policy works for the true health of its community; every time there is an act by which the wounding of our eco-system is reversed; in all these acts and many, many more God is always at work.

And Jesus entered into this ceaseless healing work of God, like a true son into the work of his father, as no other has done. 'The Son only does what he sees the Father doing', claims Jesus of his healing acts, even on the day when religious custom ordained that healing was taboo. Such a healing act, said Jesus in effect, is part of that great life-giving work of God. 'Just as the Father is himself the source of life, in the same way he has made his Son to be the source of life' (Jn 5:25). What took place in the healing of this one crippled man was to be taken as a clear sign of the new way of God - a God who is for ever a life-giving, life-healing God, and who now makes this clear in new and powerful ways.

It is as though Jesus was saying: The healing pool is right here, wherever you are. For I am here; and the healing Father is for ever at work around you. There is help at hand for you. You can walk on your own feet. The waters are being moved by the divine Spirit every day of your life, not just on odd special occasions. The healing pool is right here. The healing power of a God who gives, gives, gives eternally, is right here, right now.

IV

Finally, though, we have to return to the man who was crippled. And the story gives us a word of *warning.* Though now able to walk, all was not well with him. In a deliberate act of treacherous ingratitude, this man returns to the authorities to report to them that it was Jesus who had told him to break the Sabbath by carrying his mat. At first he had told them he did not know who had healed him - for the story says that Jesus had slipped away unnoticed as soon as he had enabled the man to get up and walk. After he'd met Jesus again, though, he could blame Jesus to the authorities for his contravening of their religious law. Strange betrayal of the one who had just healed him!

None of God's self-giving, God's healing of us, can guarantee we are now really part of God's new ways, God's new world. Jesus had cured the man to the extent of getting him to walk freely, with the strength to carry his own mat. Yet, within a short time, Jesus had to warn him to change his ways, lest some even worse condition befall him.

Along with the unending signs of God's giving and helping and healing, there are countless ways by which the inner self can be come crippled too. God's purpose is that we be enabled to overcome all that would weaken us, all that would stunt the growth of our true inner being, all that would turn us in upon ourselves, all that would make us unable to befriend others, unable to help either ourselves or others, all that would make us selfish, greedy, self-centred, unfeeling, lacking compassion — all that would cripple our true selfhood. And there are endless ways in which life can gradually cripple our true being.

To immerse ourselves, again and again and again, in the healing pool of God's ever self-giving love is where our continued healing lies. We need to open ourselves day by day to those here-and-now ways of healing, however human-seeming, however unspecial — the encouraging words of friends, the helping life of our community. Our eventual wholeness lies in continually opening ourselves to what God is able to do in such a long process of healing. Above all, we are to turn to the healing pool that is there for us in God-in-Christ, to hear his words of life, to read of his acts of love, to commit ourselves to his way of serving others; this is where our true healing lies.

12 'I Believe: Help my Unbelief'

They were coming down the mountain.... When they came to the disciples, they saw a great crowd around them, and some scribes arguing with them. When the whole crowd saw Jesus, they were immediately overcome with awe, and they ran forward to greet him. He asked them, 'What are you arguing about with them?' Someone from the crowd answered, 'Teacher, I brought you my son; he has a spirit that makes him unable to speak; and whenever it seizes him, it dashed him down; and he foams and grinds his teeth and becomes rigid; and I asked your disciples to cast it out, but they could not do so.' He answered them, 'You faithless generation, how much longer must I be among you? How much longer must I put up with you? Bring him to me.' And they brought the boy to him.

When the spirit saw him it immediately convulsed the boy, and he fell on the ground and rolled about, foaming at the mouth. Jesus asked the father, 'How long has this been happening to him?' And he said, 'From childhood. It has often cast him into the fire and into the water, to destroy him; but if you are able to do anything, have pity on us and help us.' Jesus said to him, 'If you are able! - All things can be done for the one who believes.' Immediately the father of the child cried out, 'I believe; help my unbelief!'

When Jesus saw that a crowd came running together, he rebuked the unclean spirit, saying to it, 'You spirit that keeps this boy from speaking and hearing, I command you, come out of him, and never enter him again!' After crying out and convulsing him terribly, it came out, and the boy was like a corpse, so that most of them said, 'He is dead.' But Jesus took him by the hand and lifted him up, and he was able to stand on his own (Mark 9:9,14- 27).

"I believe, but ....'

Into Your hands I commend-
Just the tips of my mind
The floss of surrender
The shooting stars
The froth of celebration;

But not the fear of wasted flesh
Not the smell of the waste-binned mind
Not the pain of foam and stress.

As one is thrown upon the ground
Not the scratching resentment
That pokes and pricks at pride.
I see dimly through cataracted eyes
And believe feebly through fractured cries
And so grip on to pain
Bolt and store up decay
Afraid to give myself away.

'I believe: help my unbelief.' 'I do have faith: help me with my doubt.' Is this not one of the most authentic human statements in the whole Bible? It expresses so convincingly the ambiguity of our life, the ambiguity of our faith. It brings out the confusing mixture of faith and doubt in the heart even of the truest followers of Jesus, the most devout lovers of God.

I had a much younger sister we used to call 'the yes-but girl'. As a child she loved to argue about things, to go on questioning even when we thought she'd been given a quite adequate answer. 'Why don't we play noisy games on Sunday?' 'Because the Bible says so', my father would say, thinking it was the last word on the matter. 'Yes, but why is Monday not special too, so that it would be wrong to go to school', would come the answer. And whatever was said, another 'yes, but' would inevitably follow.

The fact is, we are faced in life with a yes-but reality. And that's not the way most people want it. Most prefer unquestionable certainties, even in, especially in, matters of faith. And when Christians demand this of their faith they make things hard for themselves. For, so much of the Bible, so much of the gospel-stories, have this yes-but character.

Jesus, the infant in Bethlehem, born as Light for the world; yet, forced to flee because of Herod's murderous intent. Jesus, Messiah for a people oppressed; yet, groaning with frustration that even his closest followers cannot share his vision, and finding he has chosen one who is a traitor to his cause. Jesus, in Gethsemene throwing himself down in utter commitment to his Father; yet crying out to be spared the bitter cup intrinsic to such obedience. Jesus, hanging on the cross seems sure of a loving Father's approval: 'Father, into your hands I commit my spirit.' Yet, there is also that searing 'cry of dereliction', when doubt shatters the calmness of faith: 'My God, my God, why have you forsaken me?' Christians would do well to recognise that this is always how faith is: fused with deep elements of doubt.

Both for Jesus, and in Christian experience, of course, the yes-but character of things can be the other way around. Yes, there is great evil in the world; yes, there is reason to doubt; yes, things do seem hopeless.

But, God is still God. As the Apostle puts it: 'We are often troubled, but not crushed; sometimes in doubt, but never in despair; there are many enemies, but we are never without a friend; and though badly hurt at times, we are never destroyed.' For if we bear in our bodies 'the death of Jesus', then 'his life also will be seen in our bodies. (2 Cors 4:7-11).

Our story today has both kinds of yes-but ambiguity, as we shall see. The story begins on the mountain where the face of Jesus was transfigured, the place of glory where God assured Jesus that his way of suffering — lacking as it did all the certainties of other messianic ways — was the true way to God's promised world. Peter and the others wanted to stay up there in that atmosphere of divine re-assurance. But Jesus brings them down to earth again, down to a world that seemed so far removed from God. Again, as in many of these healing stories, we see the *realism* of Jesus. The experience of transfiguring was crucial to him; but it leads immediately back into that 'earthed' way of life, that engaging in the struggles, the painful, confusing realities of people's lives typical of him from the stable of Bethlehem to the cross outside Jerusalem.

I

What, then, was the situation Jesus met on his coming 'down to earth' in this story? *First*, he found a large crowd round his disciples as they were in fierce *debate* with teachers of the Jewish

Law. When he asks his disciples, 'What are you arguing with them about?', the sad story emerges of this son who was racked by such violent epileptic fits. The father of the boy had asked the disciples to heal him, but they had been unable to.

We can only conjecture as to what they were arguing about. No doubt there was the question of why Jesus' disciples had failed. This was a great chance for the religious leaders to ridicule their whole movement. As they saw it, Jesus and his group had no proper authority from God. Jesus was a fake upstart with no divine basis for his life as a preacher and healer.They even claimed that it was because he was in touch with evil powers himself that he was able to do certain kinds of healing. These acts, though, were not the sure signs from God that they demanded. No wonder they were delighted to argue about it when his disciples were impotent in the face of this more serious case.

There may even have been debate about the *reason* for such cases of suffering in children. Why is there physical pain and psychic disorder of this kind in the world? 'His parents must have sinned', is the sort of answer the religious teachers had come up with in the case of a blind man Jesus healed. Perhaps here also; it fitted their legalistic view of things. It is quite likely that Jesus' disciples were as inept at answering such arguments as they were in responding to the father's plea for healing.

II

It was, then, not only to a situation of fierce debate that Jesus re turned to: there was, *secondly*, the *disappointment* of his disciples. They had publicly failed in their attempt to respond to an appeal for help. Not only had they been inept, they had been seen to be inept by everyone there, perhaps in the ensuing debate as much as in the failed healing.

We know from a number of other incidents just how painful Jesus found it that his followers found it so hard to 'understand' the meaning either of his words or his deeds. It was as though they just could not enlarge their vision of God's ways in the world, they were just unable to stand-under this new world-view that Jesus was introducing them to. And Jesus, again and again, 'groans' at their obtuse inability to share that vision; he bemoans their 'slowness of mind' and 'hardness of heart'. 'How long must I be with you? How long must I go on struggling with you?'

And yet, there were those moments of exhilaration when they were able, in his name, to do the same things as he had been doing, to show to the world the same signs of Gods's inbreaking kingdom, and when Jesus saw 'Satan falling like a lightning-bolt from heaven'. For a long time, though, there was little but disappointment: they lacked understanding, and they were impotent to act.

On both scores the followers of Jesus in every age have usually failed him. Their response to the need for apologetic, as well as to appeals for action, have been inept. They have failed to understand the meaning of the ministry of Jesus — and so have been unable to engage in vital debate with those who ridicule all that Jesus stands for—and they have failed to respond to people's urgent needs, even those needs about which so much could be done.

Christians should, of course, always be aware of their limitations. They should not inflate their view of their own abilities, thinking they possess messianic omnipotence. As the one-time Spalding Professor at Oxford, later President of India, Sarvepalli Radhakrishna, claimed 'Christians *are* rather ordinary people making extraordinary claims.' There are many facets of the human condition about which the followers of Jesus can do little but 'fast and pray', as Jesus at the end of this story urges his disciples. Some kinds of 'healing' are in God's hands alone.

But, this still leaves vast areas of potential action for the healing of our world where we have failed even to attempt to share in what God has been doing. The followers of Jesus cause him as much pain as do those opposed to his ways. It is at least something, a step along the road of awareness, when Jesus' followers come to recognise their failure, when they share Jesus' disappointment about themselves.

And there are other kinds of disappointment in relation to healing. What are we to make of those many occasions when we pray for healing, when the doctors can do nothing, when perhaps those with a special vocation to heal lay their hands on the person in need — and it all seems to make little difference?

I read a book recently by an American Catholic healer. His contention is that if there is true faith, then we must expect exactly the healing we pray for every time hands are laid on the sick in the name of Jesus. Anything less than this is failure, failure of faith. That there should always be faith in God's healing purpose, and in God's healing power, is one thing. To demand that this be worked out exactly as we would like, is something quite different. Faith can never magically prevent 'failure' in that sense. Faith can never entirely remove disappointment, of one kind or another. Jesus knew all about such disappointment. He knew its pain. No doubt these disappointments tempered faith, they moved faith to take new directions—as is clear in the life of Jesus from time to time. Yet disappointment never broke that faith in the eternally, immovably, inexhaustibly good purpose of the Father.

III

There is a *third* ingredient in the situation confronting Jesus on coming 'down to earth': there was the painful *distress* of the father and his child. At least this must surely have tested the faith of Jesus in that good purpose of God? Great need like this seemed to have the opposite effect: it evoked even greater faith in that good purpose being able to break into the life of God's children. When asked, in another context, whether a blind man was suffering this disability because of his own sin or that of his parents, Jesus replied, 'Neither. . . This man is born blind that God's power be seen.' Or, 'because of this man's blindness, God's power is to be seen among us.' The point here is certainly not that God deliberately makes some people suffer in order that others can see how powerful he is. The point rather is this: when confronted by people in need, there we are given an opportunity for God's good purpose to break in, for his healing, helping power to be seen. This, at least, was the case when Jesus was there.

First, Jesus hears from the distraught father the full horror of his son's condition. Today most commentators describe the lad as epileptic; the sporadic convulsions, the gritting of teeth, the foaming at the mouth, the danger when fire or water are near. All are symptoms of severe epilepsy. A school-friend of mine, later when he was in his twenties, developed very serious epilepsy. It was difficult to mask the horror felt if my friend went into an epileptic fit as we were chatting together. That his wife remained so calm in the face of his uncontrollable violence, restraining him in case he did himself even more harm than was usually the case, so clearly evident from the badly scarred face and hands — her calm efficiency made me feel even more thoroughly inept, for was I not supposed to be there to give my rarely seen friend the help of my pastoral experience over and above my friendly encouragement? Inwardly, his wife too must have felt quite distraught at times.

The father's distressed concern was very natural. But does his concern also hide some deeper problem between father and son, as some recent writers have suggested? (e.g. Elisabeth Moltmann-Wendel, in *I am my Body*, a book that's full of insights relating to this healing act of Jesus). For this son is also not able to speak — even when not seized by a fit. Was the cause of his epilepsy some deep childhood trauma? Perhaps his father's excessive expectations for his son in early childhood, hopes that were so thwarted when he found his son could not speak? Certainly we are right to look at the wider web of relationships, relationships that can prove so traumatic, or so enabling, as we interact with one another — especially within the family, that closest-knit unit of all our relational life. Family life can be a great healer, or it can be that from which we need healing; it has the power to make us strong and whole, and the power to make us very fragile of psyche.

The evidence from this story is just not enough to build up a clear picture of a father's unhealthy expectation. But the strength of his distressed concern *is* clear. And he does recognise that he too is in need of Jesus' help, not just his son. 'Have pity on *us* and help *us*, if you possibly can.'

Many parents who have cared for disabled children over a long period, or children who have cared for parents, will have come to this point of despair. They become aware that their inner resources for coping with the needs of their loved one have almost been exhausted. They are near breaking-point, and their own need seems now as great as that of the disabled one. They have become one of many 'broken carers'. So this father pleads for himself as much as for his son. Whether 'broken' by too much caring or not, he is aware of his need for a new spirit, perhaps for a new relationship with this sadly dis-abled son of his.

The story describes the boy's torment as possession by an evil spirit. His own psyche, his true inner self was in the grip of some force beyond his control, a disabling, tormenting force. Just the kind of experience, in fact, that those of us who have been tormented by some inner trauma have become aware of. We find we can no longer 'be ourselves', we become subject to other compulsions far from what we would want for ourselves. As the Apostle Paul put it: 'I find I do the things I don't want to, and I cannot do the things I want to. . . . What an unhappy man I am. Who will set me free from the death I am experiencing in my body?' (Roms 7:15-25). There were forces within this boy that no one in the family could control, and that was affecting all of them. Whether there was some deep emotional trauma, an extreme form of hysteria, underlying the epileptic fits, we cannot say. All we, or the family, saw was some uncontrollable force seeming to take over this boy's body from time to time.

So, the father pleads: 'Help us, if you possibly can.' And Jesus' reply is quite extraordinary. He turns the request back on the father. 'If you *can*. Everything is possible for the person who has faith.' We have seen in other stories that Jesus certainly does not expect us to take 'everything' here in a literal sense. Did Jesus mean, for instance, that faith, even when as 'small as a grain of mustard seed', can literally uproot mountains and throw them into the sea? Obviously this was *not* his way. Did Jesus mean in a literal sense that *everything* we ask for in prayer will be granted us, just as we ask? It is such literalism that drives people, people whose faith otherwise is very real, very much in tune with the mind of Jesus, drives them to conclude that it is because of some fault in themselves, some flaw in their faith, that God does not do things just as they have prayed. The dynamism of faith in Jesus' own life worked very differently.

Yet, here Jesus says that the son's healing depends as much on the faith of the father as on his own healing power, for 'everything is possible' when there is faith. Whatever, then, lies behind this father-son relationship, or indeed the whole web of familial life of which they were part, a change in the father's attitude was called for. If he really has faith that things *can change*, they will change. There is no limit to the possibilities for healing, for wholeness in life, when there is faith in the potency of the good purpose of God to effect such changes. All kinds of new possibilities are opened up — when there is that sort of faith. It is not just that *God* then does wonderful things. For when, in the way that is intrinsic to faith, we open ourselves, our whole being, all the relationships that shape our feeling, our thinking, our capacity to love — when we open ourselves to God, we too are partners in this powerful process of healing. 'If you *can*', says Jesus. 'If you have faith, all these healing ways become possible.' The human potential to further, just as to hinder, the healing process, is limitless.

The father's response to this is quite wonderful. It comes out as a great tearing cry: 'I do have faith; help my unbelief.' This emotional outburst of the father is wonderful in its honest acknowledgement of his conflicting feelings. Hope that things can change vies with despair that nothing can be done; confidence in what Jesus says conflicts with fear that the past will still win; faith in the good purpose of God struggles with the doubt of one who has seen all too clearly and for too long how it is in the world. And this is the kind of struggle within that most of us have to work our way through: 'I do have faith; help my unbelief.'

It is a response that seems to encapsulate the inner conflict of the followers of Jesus in all their humanness. We *do* believe in his way; yet we cannot bring ourselves to that point of committing our way completely into his guiding, healing hand. We *do* believe that God's purpose for us is perfectly good, that his compassion is unlimited, that his sovereign power is great; and yet we cannot bring ourselves to be fully open to God in the way that living faith means. We *do* have faith; we also have unbelief and doubt. Our lives are so closely locked into systems and attitudes that are blatant denials of God's good purpose; and then our faith seems so feeble, such a flickering light in a threateningly dark world. But, as long as we go on crying out, with this distraught father, 'Lord, I do have faith; help my unbelief', there will continue to be all kinds of possibilities for us too. It is in the very nature of faith to struggle with doubt. Often, the doubt that leads believers to question the very tradition that nurtured us, that leads us to disturb others still quite complacent with their limited vision, to probe further into the meaning of beliefs handed on from the past, to argue even with God about the way the world seemingly always has been — such doubt can be immensely creative. In the end it can only strengthen faith, not destroy it. Doubt is not that disabling unbelief that estranges us from God, that God-denying mind-set by which we try to lock ourselves outside the 'good purpose of God'. No doubt such God-estrangement is as possible to us as God-attunement is. We are given that much power too. Most of us, though, are in that condition of tension and even conflict between faith and unbelief. And that is still a point where the healing power of God is possible.

IV

And the *final* scene of this story? The 'crowd was closing in on them.' Perhaps the effect of the 'crowd' would have been to weaken faith's struggle in this distraught father. So Jesus commands the evil force within this boy to leave him for ever. The response to this direct clash between whatever was hidden deep within this boy, whatever possessed his true self and was tormenting his whole being—the response was frightening. After violent screaming and convulsions, the boy 'looked like a corpse; and everyone said, "He is dead".' Every time this story was told and retold by the followers of Jesus in later years, they would have remembered that Jesus too had looked just like this. There was the violence of the crucifixion, the three bodies threshing in agony, then the dead corpse. 'And everyone said, "He is dead".' It was the end. God's 'good purpose' for him was finished.

But to the eyes of faith, this was not so. God took him by the hand, and raised him to new life, to a new, enhanced form of healing and helping and restoring. And for his followers, this was what was anticipated in the lifting up of this corpse-like son. 'Jesus took him by the hand, lifted him up', restoring him to new life 'standing on his own'. And also giving him a quite new 'standing' with his father. It was the healing of the life of a family as much as of this tormented boy. For the possibilities are unlimited when we open ourselves, in faith — however mixed with doubt — to the healing purpose of God.

Jyoti here in 'Wing Tips' depicts the distressed son as encased in the golden egg - another image of the life-giving sun - an image of potential new life. The bird hovers over the boy, wings outspread and holding her egg securely in place. The shape of her wings is the obverse of how the healing Bird greets the paralytic let down from the roof (in chapter 2). The son who lay 'as though dead' has to be raised up from low in the earth. And between bird and egg there is that emptiness which gives room for awakening (prabodha) *and renewal. Perhaps her wings will clap - as do birds such as the dove - to show their passion for each other. The wing-clap of the heavenly Bird will awaken and revive this son who lies 'as though dead'.*

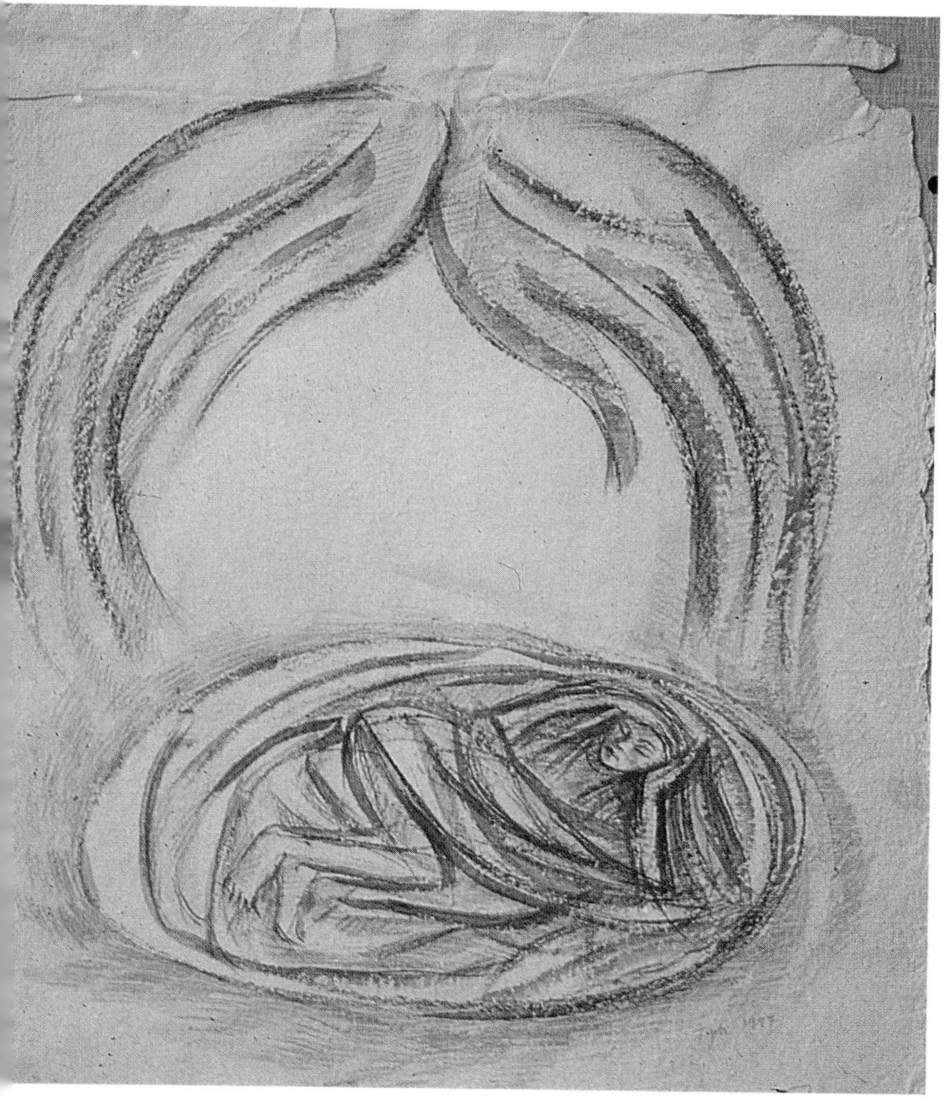

"WING TIPS"

13 ' I was Blind: Now I See'

As Jesus walked along, he saw a man blind from birth. Hid disciples asked him, 'Rabbi, who sinned, this man or his parents, that he was born blind?' Jesus answered, 'Neither this man nor his parents sinned; he was born blind so that God's works might be revealed in him. We must do the works of him who sent me while it is day; night is coming when no one can work. As long as I am in the world, I am the light of the world.' When he had said this, he spat on the ground and made mud with the saliva and spread the mud on the man's eyes, saying to him, 'Go, wash in the pool of Siloam' (which means Sent). Then he went and washed and came back able to see.

The neighbours and those who had seen him before as a beggar began to ask, 'Is this not the man who used to sit and beg?' Some were saying, 'It is he.' Others were saying, 'No, but it is someone like him.' He kept saying, 'I am the man.' But they kept asking him, 'Then how were your eyes opened?' He answered, "The man called Jesus made mud, spread it on my eyes, and said to me, "Go to Siloam and wash." Then I went and washed and received my sight.' They said to him, 'Where is he?' He said, 'I do not know.'

They brought to the Pharisees the man who had formerly been blind. Now it was a sabbath day when Jesus made the mud and opened his eyes. Then the Pharisees also began to ask him how he had received his sight. He said to them, 'He put mud on my eyes. Then I washed, and now I see.' Some of the Pharisees said, 'This man is not from God, for he does not observe the sabbath.' But others said, 'How can a man who is a sinner perform such signs?' And they were divided. So they said again to the blind man, 'What do you say about him? It was your eyes he opened.' He said, 'He is a prophet'... For a second time they called the man who had been blind, and they said to him, 'Give glory to God! We know that this man is a sinner.' He answered, 'I do not know whether he is a sinner. One thing I do know, that though I was blind, now I see.'
(John 9:1-17,24-25).

"Lead me from darkness..."

Beneath the clods of earth
On heavy long-closed lids
Something began to follow
An upward, outward surge
Towards an unseen sun;
And the eyes washed clean
Cleared and cleaved
Opened to the very source of Light.

All the Gospels present us with pictures of the sharp contrast between the old way and the new. Many of Jesus' parables depict just such contrasts in story-picture: the self-righteous Pharisee and the self-critical Publican; the Prodigal's father and his elder brother; the house built on sand and the house on rock; new wine and old bottles; and so we could go on.

Then there are the contrasts Jesus makes between his own way and the old tradition: 'Moses, and the Teachers, say this, but I say. . . .' And there is the contrast between the manner of Jesus, and those around him: his disciples, though experienced fishermen, are terrified by a sudden lake-storm; Jesus stays calmly asleep. When he taught, it was with a strangely fresh authority; not like their Teachers. As he moves around the villages, there is the constant clamour of the crowds and the chaos, even violence, of evil spirits; at the centre, Jesus remains calmly sure of God's healing power. That Jesus himself was often the cause of the agitation, and that he himself was compelled by an inner fire for God's new world, only adds to the contrast.

Of all the Gospels, John's depicts the contrast between Jesus and others most sharply. And this comes out very clearly in the story of the man blind from birth. The whole story is peppered with questions and confusion: fifteen questions in all, as though the religious leaders are no different than the common folk in their fumbling and stumbling along in the dark, 'not knowing where they were going', as Jesus put it.

Jesus, on the other hand, moves serenely through, disappearing from the scene when it pleases him, calmly detached from the crude machinations of those who sought his downfall, yet concerned for his loved ones with a consuming passion. The Gospel-writer could almost have been an Indian devotee, the style is so like that of some Indian spiritual writings. No wonder Bishop Appasamy called his reflections on this Gospel, *Christianity as Bhakti-Marga* (the 'way of love-devotion').

The climax comes in those words of sublime certainty — echoing one of the great 'I-am sayings' that have meant so much to Jesus' followers — 'While I am in the world, I am light for the world'. His words here may not have quite the declamatory force of John 8;12: 'It is *I* who am the light of the world'. But the confidence of Jesus is clear. He is sure that his way is *God's* way; his words echo *God's* words; his actions share in God's work in the world. He illumines, by all that he is and does, the lives of those who have lost direction. He gives a clear vision to those confused by life's uncertainties. Clarity, certainty, simplicity — in direct contrast to the hesitant stumbling of 'those who walk in darkness.'

I

This, then, is the *first* outstanding feature of the story of the man born blind from birth: those whose lives are open to Jesus, who are touched by his Spirit, *move from darkness into light*. They share something of the inner confidence of Jesus that life's journey is lit up by the presence and the purpose of God. Plagued by their angry questioning of what had happened, of who he believed Jesus to be, the man born blind responds with this testimony that no one could deny: 'I don't know (who he is, or what sort of person he is). One thing I do know: I was blind, and now I see. He has given me my sight.'

And this meant an *inner* vision that would go on illumining his life's path, that would enable him to see clearly what life's purpose was, enable him to *be* the person he was created to be. And because he would not betray his healer, the religious leaders curse him. Marked out as a 'disciple of Jesus', they allow him no place in their community. He is 'cast out', just as Jesus was to be out-cast for daring to challenge the darkness of their narrow ways of thinking.

One such dark way of thinking was their view that healing was wrong on the Sabbath. Again and again Jesus clashed with the authorities on this issue. He would not bow to their narrow interpretation of God's law, but persisted in healing on the holy Day of Rest. For these acts of healing were to be seen as signs of the re-creation that the Day of Rest pointed to. His was a *dynamic* view of what that Day meant. It pointed to a perfecting, a fulfilling, and therefore a restoring of everything that God intended in the great acts, the wonderful process of creation. Healing a blind man on that day was, therefore, in every way appropriate. Jesus was continuing the creative work of God, indeed, renewing that creative work.

Even the rather strange *manner* in which Jesus healed his blindness points in this same direction. 'He spat on the ground, made mud of the spittle, and smeared the mud on his eyes.' Just as humankind had been created from the earth, so the restoring and completing of creation was to be earth-related. There is another sign of this too in telling the blind man he is to wash his mud-coated eyes in the waters of the pool of Siloam. The Gospel adds that this name means 'Sent', which no doubt tells us that it is really Jesus, the 'One Sent from God', who is the 'healing pool' (as we also saw in an earlier story). He also came to be seen as the 'New Adam', that is, the new Earth-Man. Again, the God-attuned healing power of Jesus is linked with the elemental healing powers of nature; Jesus draws these earth-powers into his own healing work; as we should expect if he is continuing and restoring the work of creation.

How desperately slow the followers of Jesus have been to see this earth-dimension of Jesus' work. At last, in our time, we've been forced by the still widening ecology movement to see how wrong we've been about the natural world. We wanted to be 'modern' in our way of thinking, not held back by the superstitious ways of earlier traditions. And so we were seduced by that new world-view preached by the early fathers of modern science: nature has to be ruthlessly vanquished; she must be whipped into submission, so that her secrets can be forced from her.

This, precisely, is the kind of language used by Francis Bacon and others as they laid the foundations for a modern philosophy of science. And this violent, destructive approach to nature has been there shaping the way modernity has been treating God's creation — up to well into this past century. Suddenly, though, we've been recalled to our senses. Suddenly we realise that we have been wounding and destroying what *God has created, what God saw was 'very good'*. We have come to see that our 'salvation' is dependent on how we relate to the whole of God's creation, that we are part of the wider web of life that God has woven, and our good too lies in the good of the whole, our healing is bound up with earth's healing. Images of Jesus as the 'water of life', the 'healing pool', the 'man of earth', as well as the immense importance of the *body* and its 'salvation' in all Jesus did, point us inescapably to this more wholistic view of our human destiny.

And this changed view of things is very much a matter of those who were blind now beginning to see. It is just as though we were without sight, in the way, for so long, we have looked at creation, this precious, fragile 'home' we inhabit, this wonder-filling embodiment of the good purpose of God, this glory-throbbing expression of the life and power and loving being of God. Why, the very eyes with which we look at creation are dependent for their functioning on the light and life of the world around us. To 'see' that creation with new eyes is to see creation's God with new eyes; just as to 'see' God, and the Agent of renewal, the Agent of new creation whom God has sent, is necessarily to see creation itself with new eyes. Human healing and the healing of that creation are bound up together inextricably. The debate about the Sabbath, then, was no futile wrangling about the ritual keeping of a taboo day. Jesus affirms that healing is right and just on this day because in such healings God's creative work is to be brought to completion; and because Jesus himself is the Restorer 'sent' just for this purpose — to heal those who represent most fully God's creative purpose, and to do so *especially* on this Day meant for the re-viewing of all creation.

In John's Gospel at least this seems to be something of the meaning intended when Jesus is called 'Son of Man', as he calls himself in this story. He is not just some far-off apocalyptic figure through whom God will change things; he is the New Adam, the true

Man of Earth, the Divine Word Enfleshed, sent from heaven, from the creative heart of life, to restore to humans both a vision of their role as those who most fully embody creation within themselves, and a sense of mission as those with potential for the healing, as for the wounding, of creation's body. See things in a new way, in the way this Healer leads us, and we are already on the path to doing things in a new way. Has this not always been an essential ingredient in Indian faith? An illumined consciousness, light in the inner being, is the way by which new embodiment becomes a reality. The need to interiorise the way of Jesus, so that the healing Spirit becomes embodied within our being: this has always been very strongly affirmed in the faith of the Indian followers of Jesus. 'From darkness, lead me to light', is the ancient Indian prayer. The inner *vision, darshana*, a new way of seeing everything, insight into the true and good purpose of God in creation, is the starting point of our 'salvation'.

Jesus has shown to countless followers — perhaps by 'washing' in the 'healing pool' of baptism; but perhaps through some other 'healing pool' (for not all followers of Jesus are baptised Christians) — either way, Jesus has proved to be just this kind of illuminating darshana. But to be true to that healing which begins within, there will also be a healing ensuing in the 'body', the many interlocking relational fields, fields of energy and life, to which our inner being belongs.

II

Firstly, we turn to look at some of the changes his 'new vision' meant for this man born blind. In the *first* place, he no longer saw himself as a man cursed by God. For this was the question with which the story began: 'Whose sin caused this man's blindness ? His own or that of his parents?' Either way he was regarded as cursed by God. Jesus would have none of it. 'He is blind. . . (and) God's power will be seen at work in him'. We've looked at this text already in connection with another story. Here we can merely note again that

Jesus sees God's creative acts as still continuing; indeed, as now coming to completion; creation is being restored.

And by the end of this story, the man born blind, born cursed as far as others were concerned, is no longer cowed by a sense of curse. He witnesses clearly to his own healed condition: 'One thing I know: once I was blind, but now I see.' He speaks out clearly of the way God's good purpose works through people: 'God listens to those who respect him'. He testifies to his own faith: 'Lord, I believe', and kneels before the one who gave him this new vision. He has thrown off any inner doubt he may have had about his own worth, his acceptance to God. To be confident that we are of worth to God, that God's loving purpose is for us to throw off any debilitating sense of guilt — this too is an essential part of the healing we need.

Secondly, along with this new self-confidence, there is a critical self-awareness. This is an explicit idea brought out in John's Gospel when referring, to a person's illumining by the 'Light of the World' (e.g. 3:19-21). The Light shows us our hidden selves, the ego-flaws and inadequacies that may be painful to face up to. But how can there be inner healing unless there is complete honesty about what we really are, unless there is the insight to penetrate those carefully hidden, dark areas of our consciousness? Self-awareness alone, of course, will never lead to the healing and inner integrity we are so much in need of; merely knowing our own inadequacy could well prove the opposite of therapeutic. It could simply increase that sense of guilt from which we need healing. The 'Light', though, enables us to 'see' one who accepts us fully in spite of what we are. One who leads and supports us at every step in our struggle to be the people we long to be, and create the world we pray for. Beyond the weakness and darkness, beyond the flickering flame of our flawed ego, the Light of God remains a sure and steady healing presence.

Thirdly, those illumined by this Light find it to be an inner Light, illumining everyone coming into the world, as the Prologue of John puts it. Even if we translate with some recently as 'the Light coming into the world, illumining everyone', the sense remains the same. The Light that shone in a special way through Jesus shines also within the heart and conscience of every person on earth, however differently that illumining is experienced. The ancient Indian tradition goes one step further. Because the eternal One shines, all living things shine with that Light. Once this eternal spirit, the Light that shone through the loving life of Jesus, is discovered as our Antaryamin or Inner Controller (to use a name beloved of Indian Bhaktas), we are already on the path of inner healing.

Fourthly, with God as inner Light, a healing presence penetrating our whole being and doing, healing is to be seen as a continuing process throughout life. This is rarely made explicit in the gospel stories. There the focus is on the effective power of Jesus; but it is quite clear that each act is to be seen as but part of God's wider and continuing purpose, even within the experience of the person being healed. As healing Light shines on, there is growing awareness and experience of God's healing purpose for us.

This is one reason why it is wise to be very cautious with regard to the exaggerated claim made for instant and total healing by many 'faith-healers'. For instance, there are the extravagant claims, accepted at face-value by huge numbers of people in the United States, made by Deepak Chopra concerning the mind's power, properly directed, to cure immediately and totally almost any malfunctioning of the body and enable us to live for 130 years! Chopra draws clearly on Indian and other meditational and therapy-oriented traditions. Quite rightly we do need to recover an integration of body and soul and we do need to discover the Light within as a healing presence. That Light, though, and our healing, can never be somehow detached from the wider purpose of God for us and for the wider 'body' to which we belong. On this the mind of Jesus is clear.

Fifthly, there was the accompanying change in the authorities' perception of this blind man: from being 'the man who used to sit and beg', he became 'that fellow's disciple'. From sitting on the margins of society, there dependent only on such scraps of their life as people thought fit to throw him, he found he *belonged to a community*. As a 'disciple' of the movement around Jesus, he was first of all a 'learner', bound together with other followers in a 'discipline of learning'. He had become a *sishya*, with Jesus as his *Guru*. The term *'Guru'* is usually taken to mean 'one who banishes the darkness', and so 'one who leads into new insights'. This was

"WINGS OF LIGHT"

precisely what our blind man had experienced because of the healing action and healing word of Jesus.

Sixthly as part of this 'new insight', he came to see more of how *God discloses his mysterious purpose through Jesus.*

It is the mystery of God, however much a life-giver, that is the intention of Jyoti's 'Wings of Light'. He points to the wings of the vision of the prophets Isaiah and Ezekiel. The song of the cherubim, 'Holy, holy, holy ... Heaven and earth are full of your glory', picked up again in the book of Revelation as the song of the heavenly host, signifies the mystery of the divine presence in the eucharist by both Orthodox and Catholic worship traditions.

John's story though, began with Jesus' followers addressing him as 'Rabbi': he was seen as a teacher of some standing, able to interpret scriptures effectively, calling for no little respect in his community — though not quite as much as will be accorded a Guru. So, how far does this take us? Much of the story is the argument about Jesus between this blind man and the religious leaders. At first the man simply admits, 'I do not know where he is', 'I do not know who he is'. So there is some prompting: 'He is a sinner', because he breaks the rules of our religion with his healing on the Sabbath.

Already this blind man has seen enough to know that Jesus is compelled by concern for people rather than for rules and regulations, a concern for changing the unjust ways of the world, rather than for religious rituals. And he has seen how, along with this concern for change, he also communicates God's power to change things. He must be 'a prophet'; and is not afraid to say so. But it was in the context of being 'afraid' — which the blind man's parents were — that there is reference to Jesus as 'Messiah'. If anyone spoke of Jesus as this 'Anointed One', sent by God to bring new life to God's people, they would be thrown out from the community, pushed to the margins of life, ostracised from all the blessings of the people of God.

And this reminds us that there was no easy avoiding of confrontation and conflict in the healing way of Jesus. Where there is the inbreaking of light, there is necessarily the presence of darkness too —though 'the darkness cannot overcome the light', as was said (in the Prologue of this fourth Gospel) when affirming Jesus as the 'true light coming into the world and illumining everyone.' Jesus certainly came with the blessing of peace, *shalom*, for the world; yet he also asserts that this is not the whole story; for he also came 'to bring a sword', the sword of division resulting from the confrontation of the way of justice and truth, with the way of oppression and falsehood.

Even in the world of medical practice, often there cannot be healing without first seeming to aggravate the condition: an incision to release puss; surgery to remove a cancerous part of the body; toxic drugs to fight infection or depression; painful manipulation of a limb in chiropractice.

On this point, though, we should also note the claim of many 'alternative' ways of healing that allopathy is basically flawed in its assumption that healing is all about *fighting* whatever is seen as alien to the body. And this medical aggressiveness is parallel to those who interpret the way of Jesus almost wholly in terms of conflict with the evil they see lurking everywhere and in everyone. Even God's creation has become so corrupted by Satan that it too is now seen as the domain of the Evil One, whose demonic ways must be fought by those few believers who have been purified. Likewise, all who do not name Jesus as their only Lord and Saviour are seen as people of the Evil One.

However much some of us who follow Jesus may deeply regret this blindness — for it is blindness — to the good that is to be found both in the creative process and in many parts of our 'secular' history, as well as in the lives of many of those who do not name Jesus as their life's Guide, we are still left with the need at times for confrontation and conflict — where this is called for in order that justice be done and that healing be possible. In fact, there is even need for confrontation with those whose negatively aggressive ways so misrepresent the way of Jesus.

We cannot be like those false prophets spoken of in the Old Testament, who cried 'Peace, peace', where there is no peace; even when our deepest desire is that such peace, God's promise to us, should become a reality. The man born blind came to see clearly that he could not escape confrontation. In naming Jesus as a 'Prophet', as one who must have come from God otherwise he would not have been healed of his blindness, and then as 'Son of Man', he knew well enough he was inviting trouble. But this he accepted as part of his new life as a disciple on the road with Jesus, as he learnt each day to enlarge this new vision of the restoring of God's creation, the healing of all that has been wounded by ways of evil. 'I was blind; now I see.'

14 Lazarus

Now a certain man was ill, Lazarus of Bethany, the village of Mary and her sister Martha. Mary was the one who anointed the Lord with perfume and wiped his feet with her hair; her brother Lazarus was ill. So the sisters sent a message to Jesus, 'Lord, he whom you love is ill.' But when Jesus heard it, he said, 'This illness does not lead to death; rather it is for God's glory, so that the Son of God may be glorified through it.' Accordingly, though Jesus loved Martha and her sister and Lazarus, after having heard that Lazarus was ill, he stayed two days longer in the place where he was.

Then after this he said to the disciples, 'Let us go to Judea again.' The disciples said to him, 'Rabbi, the Jews were just now trying to stone you, and are you going there again?'. Jesus answered, 'Are there not twelve hours of daylight? Those who walk during the day do not stumble, because they see the light of this world. But those who walk at night stumble, because the light is not in them.' After saying this, he told them, 'Our friend Lazarus has fallen asleep, but I am going there to awaken him.' The disciples said to him, 'Lord, if he has fallen asleep, he will be alright.' Jesus, however, had been speaking about his death, but they thought he was referring merely to sleep. Then Jesus told them plainly, 'Lazarus is dead. For your sake I am glad I was not there, so that you may believe. But let us go to him.' Thomas, who was called the Twin, said to his fellow disciples, 'Let us also go, that we may die with him.'

When Jesus arrived, he found that Lazarus had already been in the tomb four days. Now Bethany was near Jerusalem, some two miles away, and many of the Jews had come to Martha and Mary to console them about their brother. When Martha heard that that Jesus was coming, she went and met him, while Mary stayed at home. Martha said to Jesus, 'Lord, if you had been here, my brother would not have died....' Jesus said to her, 'I am the resurrection and the life. Those who believe in me, even though they die, will live... Do you believe this?' She said to him, 'Yes, Lord, I believe that you are the Messiah, the Son of God, the one coming into the world.'

When she had said this, she went back and called her sister Mary, and told her privately, 'The Teacher is here and is calling for you.' And when she heard it, she got up quickly and went to him... When Mary came where Jesus was and saw him, she knelt at his feet and said to him, 'Lord, if you had been here, my brother would not have died.' When Jesus saw her weeping, and the Jews who came with her also weeping, he was greatly disturbed in spirit and deeply moved. He said to them, 'Where have you laid him?' They said to him, 'Lord, come and see.' Jesus began to weep. So the Jews said, 'See how he loved him!' But some said, 'Could not he who opened the eyes of the blind man have kept this man from dying?' Then Jesus, again greatly disturbed, came to the tomb. It was a cave, and a stone was lying against it. Jesus said, 'Take away the stone.' Martha, the sister of the dead man, said to him, 'Lord, already there is a stench because he has been dead four days.' Jesus said to her, 'Did I not tell you that if you believed, you would see the glory of God?' So they took away the stone. And Jesus looked upward and said, 'Father, I thank you for having heard me. I knew that you always hear me, but I have said this for the sake of the crowd standing here, so that they may believe that you sent me.' When he had said this, he cried out with a loud voice, 'Lazarus, come out!' The dead man came out, his hands and feet bound with strips of cloth, and his face wrapped in a cloth. Jesus said to them, 'Unbind him, and let him go.' (John 11:1-44).

The Further Shore

The end
Is very like the beginning:
A waiting for delivery.
A crystal being, shaped and dressed,
Slowly coloured by
A life's experience.
Preparing for a life
within another space
And time and light,
He lies on open
No-man's land
In transit
But conscious

Of the borders,
Open-eyed, dry -lipped.
He has no strength
To move or speak.
He hovers on raw edges
Waiting, dry waiting
For another hand
To carry him across.

Today's story is perhaps the most remarkable 'healing' in the New Testament. It tells us of the death of Lazarus and his being brought back to life by Jesus after he'd been buried four days. Of all the healing stories, this is the most 'miraculous'. Even those who would not want to take this in a literal sense, but rather as a kind of parable of the new life after death that is now promised through Jesus, are still left with the need for miracle; if, by 'miracle', we mean an act or a phenomenon that breaks through, that transcends, that cannot be explained by some natural order of things. For, any kind of 'resurrection' is a miracle; but then, so is the gift of life in the first place. In fact I'm inclined to believe that the life I have now is a greater miracle, less explicable by some 'natural order of things', than is the life I hope will somehow be given hereafter. Whether, then, we feel the need to take this story literally or not, we must in any case focus on the 'miracle' to which it points. 'Your brother will rise to life', is how this is put initially. Then it is said in terms of faith in Jesus: 'Whoever believes in me will live, even though he dies.' These are words from a passage read in public — at funerals — throughout the world where there are Christians, probably more often than any other piece of religious writing the world has known. What does the story say to us?

I

The background to the story is the *close companionship* of Jesus and this family at Bethany — Mary, Martha and Lazarus. Lazarus is described as a 'dear friend' of Jesus. It is said that Jesus 'loved Martha and her sister and Lazarus.' But it is *Mary* who seems to have established the closest relationship of the three with Jesus. There was a deep spiritual intimacy between them. She it was, according to John's story, who had poured costly perfume on to the feet of Jesus, as well as washing them with her tears and wiping them with her hair. Clearly she was a woman given to extravagant gestures of feeling. But Jesus would not allow her to be criticised for wasting what could have been given to the poor. She had, he said, shown a deep insight into what his destiny was. The anointing of his body she had given him was a pointer to the self-sacrifice he was soon to make; and she would always be remembered for this act of devotion.

Then there was the time when Jesus and his followers had arrived en route for Jerusalem. Food had to be prepared; but it was all left to Martha to do. Mary, 'sitting at the feet of the Lord', was too deeply engrossed in what he was saying. Again, Jesus did not accept Martha's criticism: Mary had, rightly, 'chosen the one thing that was needed'. There was that single-minded devotion about her, that 'attentiveness' Eastern faiths see as crucial to spiritual progress, there was that passion to learn more of the mind of Jesus and give herself wholly to this 'one thing' so prized by *bhakti*, as well as by Jesus.

Martha was more the matter-of-fact pragmatist, the kind of person who made sure things were done, and done well, who wanted things to be under control. There was not only the matter of the cooking. She it was who voiced her doubt when Jesus asked them to roll away the tomb-stone. 'But he's been buried four days. Decay will have set in long since.' Yet, Martha is the first to affirm strongly her faith in Jesus: 'Yes, Lord; I do believe that you are God's Anointed, the Son of God, the One to come into the world (from God)'. Even her faith is well-controlled, clearly articulated. She's a bit of a theologian; Mary more of a mystic, intuiting her deep-felt convictions.

Little is known of Lazarus — except that he was a 'dear friend', and that later he was marked out for death by the religious authorities, because he was so closely identified with the success of Jesus. All in all, it was a very mixed family.

Yet, we are left in no doubt about the closeness of the bond between this family and Jesus. There may well have been other such families, in the wide range of friends Jesus had, with whom there was an equally close companionship. But we are not told of them. That Jesus was an outstandingly companionable person, able to make friends of and enjoy greatly his friendship with all kinds of people, is made very clear. It was a matter of particular offence to those whose religiosity was so very different; those Pharisees for whom the word 'uptight' seems tailor-made. How could anyone, they muttered, with pretensions to being a Rabbi, also be a 'friend of tax-collectors and sinners', with those who should be treated as social untouchables, national traitors, and religious infidels? No wonder they clashed so sharply, Jesus and the Puritans of his time. Yet Jesus was one who revelled in the companionship of that Bethany family.

II

The *second* insight into the mind of Jesus that we gain from this story is from the degree of *compassion* he showed when faced with the death of his friend and the mourning of the sisters. It is true that there is a strange reticence at first to go to Bethany where Lazarus was said to be sick. He assures people that it will not end with the death of Lazarus, but with the glory of God. Even when Lazarus was dead, Jesus affirms: 'Our friend Lazarus has fallen asleep; but I will go and wake him up,' (in a way reminiscent of the little daughter of Jairus). His disciples are comforted to hear that Lazarus is 'asleep', but not at all happy to hear that Jesus intends to go to the region where his life was in peril. It is only when you're not walking 'in the light of day', says Jesus, that there is fear of stumbling and falling. So they set off for Bethany. And they are met by Martha (Mary staying at the house, deeply traumatised by the death of her brother, and by the failure of Jesus to save him). Both sisters, first Martha, later Mary, greet Jesus with the same distraught lament: 'If only you had been here. . .' How often death, especially those deaths we call 'untimely', are met with this same lament: 'If only. . . .' 'If only we had done this'. 'If only there had been more time'. 'If only. . . .' And behind this lament lies another one: '*Why* did God allow this to happen?' '*Why* did God not save our loved one?' '*Why* did God not come to our help when we called to him?'

glory, an illumining of life, will be manifest in and through this dark place of mourning. Then comes his witness to his own direct role in bringing this tinge of glory even to the grave: 'I am the resurrection and the life. . .' When there is faith, when there is openness of heart and life to all that Jesus does and says and *is*, his follower finds that death is no longer a dark valley by which all hope is extinguished. It is no longer merely the *end* of life; it becomes an opening, a doorway, a beginning of new life.

So he commands them: 'Take the stone away'; 'Remove that by which we block out death, our age-old fears, our heavy traumas, our deep-rooted unconscious anxieties — all that prevents us from coming face to face with our real and lonely selfhood in all its dark, frightening, tomb-clasped mortality. We are finite creatures. And there is no hope for us until we acknowledge, gladly and unreservedly, this finite, tomb-cramped nature of ours. Remove this blocking-stone, says Jesus, and make it a doorway instead.

In fact, it is at the centre of the faith of the followers of Jesus that a death of our old self — with its confused fear and pride, its guilt and its greed, its self-loathing and its self-serving — a death of that old self is needed before there can be healing and new life. But then — then Jesus can point us to the hope of *new creation*, the hope that we ' *will rise to life*', the hope of sharing in the new inbreaking of God's renewing power, the hope of 'seeing God's glory' even at that point of tomb-like darkness when all seems lost.

Then, when the stone was rolled away, and all they could expect was the stench of death, Jesus 'called out with a loud voice, "Lazarus, come out!" And he came out, hands and feet and face bound by grave clothes.' Like a butterfly, unrecognisable in the ugly confines of its chrysalis-clothes, eager for the buoyant uplifting of life on the wing, Lazarus shuffled out from his dark tomb, lurching into the light.

For him, the tomb had been a second womb, as he awaited new birth. And is not the extreme weakness of sickness, or of old age, for many people like a regression to a womb-like existence? Unable to do anything for themselves, having to accept again their dependence on the caring and nursing of others, perhaps having to accept the indignity of being incontinent and the frustration of being unable to

Jesus' response to Martha was by way of promise: 'Your brother will rise to life.' Then comes that great 'I-am' affirmation: 'I am the resurrection and the life. Whoever believes in me will live, even though he dies. . .' And Martha is persuaded: 'Yes, Lord; I do believe. . .' His response to Mary was different. When he saw her weeping, along with other mourners weeping with her, it is said: 'His heart was touched, and he was deeply moved'. And the next verse is the most terse in scripture: 'Jesus wept'. Mary then invites Jesus to 'come and see' where their brother was buried. And again, as they came near to the cave-tomb, he was 'deeply moved once more'. 'See how much he loved him!', they all exclaimed.

Nowhere is the pain-sharing compassion of Jesus expressed so vividly. Nowhere are we given a more open window into the heart of Jesus—except, of course, when we come to his self-giving on the cross. But we have to interpret that cross, the meaning of his death, in the light of such soul-exposing incidents as this one beside the cave-tomb of his friend Lazarus. When we say that by becoming incarnate Jesus shared our life, we find these moments of compassion leading us one step further.

In the pain of his cross we see the compassionate, pain-sharing heart of God most clearly. There is no human suffering, maybe we should say no creaturely suffering, in which God does not share. Just as Jesus had been there with his friends, joining in their laughter, indeed the cause of their hilarity of spirit, so he is there at the graveside, weeping for his friend, weeping with his friends. So too *God* is there, sharing in the pathos as well as the rapture of life. And with the heart of pure love that is God's, compassion moves God to feel far more than we ever can the suffering of others; even our own pain moves the heart of God to a suffering that is beyond what we could bear. But the only 'proof' of this pain-sharing heart of God are the signs of compassion we see in Jesus.

III

Thirdly, though, along with the compassion there is a quiet *com posure*. The concern of Jesus is not the distraught lamenting of other mourners at the grave; there is a quiet confidence that God's

"LIFE BEARER"

communicate, they regress further and further into infancy. In death they slip back into the waters of the womb, the womb of our mortal being. The miracle that brought us to life in that first birth is not merely repeated. Rather, we are pointed to a life-giving miracle, a new birth, that now transforms us into the life of the eternal world. 'From this mortal being, lead me into the immortal world', is the prayer of ancient India. And this story in John's Gospel shows Jesus leading his followers to just such an immortal stage of being. 'I am the resurrection and the life. Those who believe in me will live, even though they die. . .'

In a number of sacred stories and icons of India, a bird is portrayed as the semi-divine carrier (vahana) ***of sacred figures (Golden Garuda carries Vishnu, the Peacock carries Murugan, the Swan carries Sarasvati, goddess of the arts and music). Jyoti here in 'Life Bearer' shows the soul being carried on the wings of the heavenly bird, carried across the waters to the 'further shore'. The journey is not smooth and easy; so the bird itself is like a fiery vortex, into whose churning movement the soul is caught up.***

And the new birth that was described of Lazarus, or the new birth that we are to expect from our old cast-off selfhood, in this life of faith and following, are powerful pointers to the final new birth God promises, when the tomb becomes a second womb. At the tomb of Lazarus, Jesus was the mid-wife, 'with a loud voice' urging the unborn child out to its new life.

'Unbind him; let him go free', was the order he gave when Lazarus shuffled out of his tomb. This is a hint of the liberation for which we long — in life and in death.

In recent years this word 'liberation' has taken on a whole new range of meaning for the followers of Jesus. If we take our following seriously at all, we now find we are compelled to struggle for the 'unbinding' of people from every kind of structure — be it social, or political, or economic, or cultural, or psychological — every kind of organised life that oppresses life, that curtails our humanness.

Because we *know* that Jesus calls us out into the freedom of new life, God-promised new life.

And anything that opposes that liberated life must itself be opposed. The struggle to understand and be faithful to the nature of the struggle is itself crucial to our faithful following of Jesus. But we hear his command: 'Unbind him; let her go free.' And so we seek to obey the word of Jesus, according to the special vocation, the special calling each has. For we see this liberating process — the unbinding of bodies here: the social body, the body politic, the eco-body — as essential to the enriching of selfhood, the breaking in of new life, that we long for in the personal being of every one of God's children. 'Unbind them; let them go free.' Or, as that stirring spiritual of the Black People of America put it: 'Let my people go!' - Set my people free! Let my people be!

There is one other story in the Gospels (Luke 16:19-31) of a poor man called Lazarus. He too was healed. In life, sores covered his body; the dogs came to lick them. Lazarus sat at the door of a wealthy man's house, hoping for scraps to eat. But when he died, all was transformed: Lazarus reclined 'on the bosom of Abraham', rejoicing in a life of pleasant luxury. The rich man, though, was in painful torment. He was also tormented by the thought that his five brothers needed to be warned of what awaited them; so, could Lazarus be sent to them? But the story goes on to say 'they would not be convinced even if someone were to rise from death' and go to them to tell them they must change their unjust way of life. If they don't see the need for such change when they are challenged by all the prophetic voices there have already been, what is there that will get them to change?

'Lazarus' means 'a man with none to help', and therefore a man without hope. But in both these stories of one with this name, the hope of change, the hope of a new life, a new future, the hope of liberation, of being set free from all that fetters, of being healed of all that wounds and causes pain — life-changing hope is affirmed. And every follower of Jesus is promised a share in the miracle by which we are enabled to live out this life-changing hope.

15 Look, Listen, Live

One day Peter and John were going up to the temple at the hour of prayer, at three o'clock in the afternoon. And a man lame from birth was being carried in. People would lay him daily at the gate of the temple called the Beautiful Gate so that he could ask for alms from those entering the temple. When he saw Peter and John about to go into the temple, he asked them for alms. Peter looked intently at him, as did John, and said, 'Look at us.' And he fixed his attention on them, expecting to receive something from them. But Peter said, 'I have no silver or gold, but what I have I give you; in the name of Jesus of Nazareth, stand up and walk.' And he took him by the right hand and raised him up; and immediately his feet and ankles were made strong. Jumping up, he stood and began to walk, and he entered the temple with them, walking and leaping and praising God; and they recognised him as the one who used to sit and ask for alms at the Beautiful Gate of the temple. And they were filled with wonder and amazement at what had happened to him.

While he clung to Peter and John, all the people ran together to them in the portico called Solomon's Portico, utterly astonished. When Peter saw it, he addressed the people, 'You Israelites, why do you wonder at this, or why do you stare at us, as though by our own power or piety we had made him walk? The God of Abraham, the God of Isaac, and the God of Jacob, the God of our ancestors has glorified his servant Jesus, whom you handed over and rejected in the presence of Pilate, though he had decided to release him. But you rejected the Holy and Righteous One and asked to have a murderer given to you, and you killed the Author of life, whom God raised from the dead. To this we are witnesses. And by faith in his name, his name itself has made this man strong, whom you see and know; and the faith that is through Jesus has given him this perfect health in the presence of you all... Repent therefore, and turn to God so that your sins may be wiped out, so that times of refreshing may come from the presence of the Lord, and that he may send the Messiah appointed for you, that is, Jesus, who must remain in heaven until the time of universal restoration that God announced long ago through his holy prophets (Acts 3:1-21).

The Leap to Life

Sure footed he leapt
Unwearied he sang
And he praised, as he walked
To the temple; he sang
O Lord of the leaping
Sure-stepping deer,
Shake off the dust
Of our beggarly fear,
The shifting and shuffling,
The starting and sticking,
Oh wait for and catch us
As we pass over, risking
The leap to full life.

My title sounds a bit like a warning sign at a railway crossing: 'Look, and listen, if you want to live'. The story that prompts these three words — look, listen, live —is far from a warning, or cautionary tale. And yet, in the words of Peter that follow the healing, there is a mixed message. It's full of promise; but there's also a sharp warning edge to his words.

It's the first story we've reflected on that is not from the Gospels; it is not, on the face of it, a healing by Jesus. Yet, that is precisely what Peter claims for this healing act: it is the risen Jesus still at work, still carrying out his mission of healing. Now, though, he is doing what he did before, through the 'acts of his apostles', those 'sent' with precisely this mandate: to share in the work he had 'begun to do and say', as the author of Acts puts it. The story is set in the time very soon after Pentecost. So the clear meaning is that the strange overshadowing with licking tongues of fire and the strong whistling wind must never be taken as something separate from the known ways and the manifest mind of Jesus. It was the Spirit of Jesus, the Spirit of the 'God and Father' of Jesus, that was now empowering the Apostles of Jesus.

I

But what about these three Ls - Look, Listen, Live? How are they part of the story? *First*, then, there is the story's emphasis on *looking*. The opening scene is of Peter and John going to the Temple for prayer. When they came to the 'Beautiful Gate', they came across a man sitting and begging, a sight we're introduced to in a number of healing stories, as we have seen. It's still a common sight at countless temple gates in India; it's an increasingly common sight at the entrance to public places — especially Underground stations — in the big cities of Britain. When there's a growing gap between haves and have-nots, between affluence and poverty, there's always a growing number of people reduced to begging as a way of life. It's never merely a matter of lazy cadgers making a living from the goodwill of the weak-minded and soft-hearted.

So this man asks Peter and John for money. A begging man will be quite used to people reacting to his cries for help with total indifference; looking through him as though he just does not exist. Beggars will also be used to the careless throwing of a small coin. And if they are over-insistent in their begging, they will be used to irritated curses. But these Apostles of Jesus respond quite differently.

First, 'they looked straight at him'. Unlike the vast majority of those who passed him, they actually *saw* him. They saw him as a human being. They saw him as a child of God. They saw him as he could be, as he *should* be. They saw him not as an ugly disfigured beggar, but as the beautiful creature God intended, there at the Beautiful Gate of God's Temple. They looked directly at the true personhood of this man, his true being obscured by his rags, his smell, his crippled state, his beggar's whine. For the way we see people is so conditioned by the outer shell of their being — what the Indian theological tradition would call the mere 'name and form' of things, rather than the inner reality, the hidden embodied self within. To *see* that inner being we need the new vision pointed to in the previous story. Peter and John saw this disabled beggar with just such new vision. Other gospel stories tell us that we are to *see* every person just as though they were Jesus himself before us. In the Song of the Lord, the Bhagavad Gita, also we're told in a general way (by Krishna) to 'see me in everything, and everything in me'. Jesus is more specific: If you feed the hungry, clothe the naked, give drink to the thirsty, help the sick, visit those in prison, you are doing it to me. So do not say, 'When, Lord, did we see you hungry, naked, thirsty. . . .' When you see the needy, you see me. When you give just a cup of water to 'the most insignificant' of my brothers and sisters, you are doing it to me. We are to see *Jesus* in the poor, the vulnerable, those least noticed by others.

The 'direct look' of a person also has another significance. It is felt, in folk traditions, that there is strange *power* in a person's look. The eye is the point at which all a person's potency is concentrated; the eye focuses things in more ways than one. If that look has evil intent, there is an 'evil eye'. And the look of an evil spirit has power to curse, to draw the life out of a person, the power to kill. But in a similar way, the look of God is powerful — potent both to bless and to punish. God is often depicted as the 'all-seeing eye'. And the prayer of the desperate will be: 'Look on me, Lord, look on me for good'. There are many prayers like this in the Psalms.

The deliberately direct look of Peter and John, therefore, is a way of focusing all the healing intent they have for this disabled beggar. Just like the touch of a healer's hands, whether a doctor or some other healer, the touch of the eye is also a potent pre-disposing factor in the healing process. Those doctors who, increasingly, look only at their computer screen when their patient is with them have missed something important in the healer-patient relationship.

Then the Apostles ask this man to relate to them in the same way: 'Look at us!' Eye-contact is a two-way affair. The disabled beggar too must look directly and deliberately at them. Two meanings come to mind here. First, social pressures would demand that this man did *not* look directly at his 'superiors'. I remember how disconcerting I found it in my early years in India when meeting certain kinds of people, perhaps on a quite narrow path, and they would just not look at me even when I greeted them with a genial '*namaskaram*'. It took a while to realise that women, 'menials', tribals, and others, like beggars, expected to see themselves as 'inferior', were conditioned by society *not* to look directly at their 'betters'. Peter and John have to counter this with a direct command: 'Look at us!'

Then, too, a focused eye-contact was needed that at least the beginnings of a *relationship* be formed between them. Healing always has a relational dimension, for it needs to involve the whole person — of the one to be healed as well as the healer. At least the healing, the wholeness, of which the Gospel stories speak, aim to touch and transform the whole being of the person in need. But this healing process also calls for the focusing of the intention of the one whose life is to be changed. A degree of 'attention' is needed, even if this is not the rigorous concentration of mind that classical systems of spirituality expect as the starting-point on the path of inner illumination. 'Look at us', urged the Apostles. This is your first step in finding a new direction for your life.

Very soon, of course, this focused look will need to go further; it will need to be the sharing of the same vision, being gripped by the same view of God's purpose for a sick and wounded world. By then, of course, this needy man will have come to realise that the Apostles are not saying merely 'Look *at us*!' They are rather saying: 'Look *through us*, look at the One who is the Source of all healing and of all blessing'. So we find that as soon as the crowd come running in amazement at this act of healing, Peter challenges their perception of what had happened: 'Why do you stare at *us*? Do you think it was by means of our own power or godliness that we made this man to walk?' But this takes us on to our next point.

II

The *second* major theme in the story is summed up by the word '*Listen*'. In the first place the Jewish people, gathered there at their Temple, were asked to listen to their own story. There's reference to Abraham and all the patriarchs, Moses and 'all the prophets who had a message'. Even from biblical times people have been asking in some astonishment, why *this* history? 'How odd/ of God/ to choose/ the Jews!' Yet, the Apostles were sure that in this strange and tortuous history of God's dealings with the people of

Israel, an amazing journey of faith, and of unbelief, there are compelling insights into the way God, patiently and relentlessly, had been seeking to lead them to freedom.

These stories from Israel's past were, of course, seen as leading up to something special. Throughout that history, claimed Peter, there were clues pointing to 'the Prophet to be sent', the 'Messiah who had to suffer', the 'Servant, given divine glory, who would bless all people on earth', the 'time for all things to be made new'. And it was the Jesus who was rejected by you, and killed under Pilate, to whom all these clues point. So, then, '*listen*' to this story of Jesus.

'Listen', urged the Apostle, to this *Name, the Name of Jesus*. When the beggar at the gate had asked for alms, Peter replied that he had none. Strictly speaking this was probably not the case; all the believers had pooled everything they owned, to be used for the common good. Some of this was no doubt set aside for needy cases of this kind. Yet, what Peter offered this disabled beggar was not money, but the healing power of the Name. Here was something very specific to focus his attention on, to focus his hopes on, to find a new future through. The Name of Jesus; its literal meaning being 'one who saves', 'one who heals'.

There's nothing new to religious people in India about faith in a Name. Many of the songs of intense devotion sung by followers of Rama, Krishna, Guru Nanak, and many other *bhakti* traditions, are focused on 'the Name'. For the Name serves to embody all the sacred qualities of power and love of the concerned divine figure. Focusing on 'the Name', repeating it again and again, interiorising it so that the Name fills all thinking and feeling, serves to bring the whole person of that God close to the devotee, strengthening the sense of that divine Lover's intimate presence within the heart of the beloved disciple. And Peter here speaks of the Name of Jesus as embodying all the loving presence and all the healing power of the risen Lord.

Clearly there are dangers here of using the Name as a magic formula. Though Jesus himself seemed quite unbothered when told of a man who was using his name to heal, later in Acts we're told of the seven sons of Sceva trying this ploy and being violently attacked by the one with the evil spirit they were exorcising, so that they had to run off 'wounded and with their clothes torn off.' Magic was unacceptable. So the new believers of Ephesus brought all their books of magic and burnt them in public — their value equal to the huge amount of around 100 years worth of rural wages. Strange, though, that those who carried off, to perform cures, the handkerchiefs that Paul had used — maybe even to blow his nose!—seem to be approved by the writer of Acts. Which surely serves to remind us that we can be very inconsistent in our ideas of what constitutes 'superstitious magic'.

But there is a far more serious point to ponder here. Peter affirmed very forcefully that 'it was the power of the Name of Jesus that gave strength to this disabled man. . . It was faith in Jesus that made him whole, as you can all see.' But what are we to make of the claim by Peter, made before the all-important Jewish Council when they were brought in for questioning about this healing, the claim that 'salvation is to be found through (this Name) alone; in all the world there is no one else God has given to save us'?

Very clearly God has in fact given many other 'names'; prophets, mystics, God-lovers, divine figures, spiritual guides, healers, helpers, story-tellers, bridge-builders, counsellors, bread-providers, charismatic community leaders — all who 'at sundry times and in sundry places' have become names to invoke as the focus for so many different kinds of blessing to the human race. There are many religious communities other than those confessing the Name of Jesus, in which people have experienced various forms of 'salvation': inner, as well as bodily, healing; a sense of sharing in God's love and goodness; confidence that their eternal destiny is assured.

I recall the impact made in my life by a book I read in 1958, with exactly the title of the Hebrews' verse quoted above — *At Sundry Times*, by the Spalding Professor at Oxford, R.C. Zaehner. A convinced Catholic, Zaehner was equally sure that God's saving purpose is revealed in religious traditions that know nothing of the Name of Jesus. When Peter speaks of 'all the prophets', each having a story with which to enrich the whole story of God's purposes, there is no way we can exclude 'prophets' of other faiths, other cultures making up the great global family of God.

It was at the 'Beautiful Gate' of the Temple of the Jewish people that healing was found by this disabled beggar. But there are many other places, people, prayers, songs, ways of life in many other religions that are 'beautiful', though not 'Christian'. We should rejoice in them; rejoice that God's loving purpose is so inclusive, embraces so many different kinds of people.

What, then, is so special about this Name? Is it not that, for those who have shared in the saving, healing, loving purpose at work through Jesus — embodied in his Name — there is an irrepressible conviction that this is a very distinctive kind of saving, healing, loving? It is a very *peculiar* kind of purpose that is found herein. And there is 'no salvation', no healing, of this *particular kind* 'given by God by anyone else in the world'. But this conviction should never erase respect, even love, for other Names, other 'ways' of salvation. In my own vocation from God, indeed, I have been given as a major task in life the work of struggling to find meeting-points, as well as points of departure, between such differing faiths and differing Names. I have no doubt whatsoever that this is a vocation that has been blessed by the Jesus whose Name I especially love and whose power I believe in.

In other words, we are to learn to *listen*, listen to the wonderfully varied voices of people whose experience of life, and whose cultural styles, may be very different from our own. For, as Jesus assures us, *God* certainly listens to every voice lifted up in the urgency of human need, or in the ecstasy of divine worship. God certainly listens to every voice speaking to another from a heart of genuine love. And because *God* listens, we are to learn to listen, listen to what people actually have to say to us, whether they be people sharing faith and life, or people seeking healing. Sometimes this means listening to the hidden plea behind the surface words. It was at this deeper level that Jesus always listened, listened so carefully to what people had to say, in some cases questioning and probing further into their more hidden selfhood.

Learning really to listen is so difficult for us. Yet the crucial role of the listener has been one of the most important advances in the modern understanding of mental health and counselling. Few medical practicioners, however, have developed this basic skill, often from lack of time, but sometimes from lack of that humility which recognises the importance of the patient's role in the healing process. In reality no healer can ever be effective without this willingness to listen.

III

The *third* major theme of this story is summed up in the word *live*. 'Look, listen, and live!' Peter makes a sharp contrast between 'the one who leads to life', and the violent killing to which the priestly leaders had condemned him: 'You killed the one who leads to life'; one who 'was holy and good', 'you rejected, and instead (asked for) a murderer'. Jesus is depicted in striking contrast with both life-destroying leaders and life-destroying Barabbas. There is even a third contrast: 'You killed the one who leads to life, but God raised him from death (to resurrection life).'

The irony is that these 'killers' were not especially evil men. But they had such pride in their ancient tradition, such a natural love for their priestly status and all the privileges granted by Roman rule, and such a natural fear of any change in the *status quo*, that they were quite sure Jesus had to be done away with. He was too great a threat to the system, to the peaceful ordering of their community. Their greed for continuity and the benefits of priestly life may have been 'natural', but it was in the end murderous. It led them to a blind blocking of the new way that God was opening up through Jesus.

Even for them, though, Peter announces that new life is possible. It was because they did not understand — people and leaders alike — that they did away with 'the one who leads to life'. So there is still the chance to change, to turn to God, to be forgiven. The word usually translated 'repentance' here, literally means 'change of mind'; it means an inner U-turn, so that the whole of life is opened up to God.

Then, says Peter, 'If you do, there will come opportune times for recovery from the presence of the Lord', and eventually 'the time when all things are made new, as God announced through the prophets.' Again, it is worth noting the literal meaning of this term 'recovery' — in any case hinting at the *healing* of life. It is the *psyche* that is referred to here, the renewal of the psyche, meaning the whole life and (literally) breath of the human being. There is to be an inner recovery that will then lead on to the renewal of everything in creation.

Much is made, in the story of the disabled beggar's healing, of the way, helped up by Peter's hand-grasp, he was able to 'stand on his own feet', and was then leaping and bounding with the new strength of body he'd received. Here too is a pointer to the prophetic promise that the 'lame would leap and dance'(Isaiah 35:6) as part of that cosmic transforming when 'streams of water will flow through the desert... and the dry land will be filled with springs'. So this beggar at the Temple stood as a pointer to something far greater than just the healing of one man. It pointed to the time we can hope for and work for when everything in God's creation will share in the promised 'recovery' of life, when (as Peter put it) Jesus will prove to be a 'blessing to all people on earth'. For did not this 'Good Shepherd' say of his life's work, 'I have come that you might have *life, life in all its fulness*' (John 10:10)?

I close, though, with a further look at the new liveliness of the healed beggar, seen in his 'leaping and dancing'. Crippled people do not dance. That this one does, of course, is what points dramatically to the miraculous power at work here. His dancing expresses the overflowing joy he felt at being made whole. For healing means the attunement of body and spirit, when the body is able to give full expression to the inner life of the restored soul, spoken of as the work of the Good Shepherd in Psalm 23.

This means, then, that the reverse is also true: dance can also help in the healing process; it can be therapeutic. Indeed, all *play*, all play that is truly recreational as play is intended to be, has healing potential. It is no less than tragic that so much of our sport today seems merely to bring out a spirit of self-destructive greed, or macho viciousness, rather than being a playful overflow of that comradely spirit — even if a competitive comradely spirit — as play is meant to be.

True play will also include those 'unproductive' ways of being human such as drama, art, story-telling, comedy and clowning,

"WINGED DANCE"

singing and music, and certainly dance. All can be therapeutic. But if, for example, we dance only because it helps to keep the body fit, or just as a way of meeting people of the other sex, or because our peer group tells us it's the thing to do, we sadly miss the point. Whether formal in style, or the spontaneous leaping of the beggar moved by an upsurge of joy at being made whole, dance expresses the essential playful spirit of being human. When we cease to play, we are less than human. Such truly self-expressive activity, therefore, will always help in some way to restore lost wholeness.

Indian spirituality, both primal and classical, has often seen the very character of God in the image of the dancer — dancing Nataraj, dancing Ganapati, dancing Krishna, the three-stepping Vamana, various folk-heroes. God as *drummer* too is a striking image in the Indian, as well as African, primal consciousness. It is even through God's *lila*, God's dancing playfulness, that all creation takes place. If creativity is essentially playful dance, recovery of the wholeness of creation, as of our own bodily being, will surely in part depend upon our recovery of the playful spirit of the dancer. Jesus in one sense *danced* his way through Galilee's villages, danced his way even to Golgotha's cross; for he came to bring 'life in all its fulness', and his acts of healing draw us — sometimes playfully, sometimes painfully - into that fulness of being, the wholeness of being for which he lived, died and rose to new life again. Jyoti Sahi has at least 20 paintings. Many Jesus and his disciples dancing.One of his most potent paintings is of the risen Jesus, body resplendent in resurrection glory, dancing his way across the sleeping towns and villages of an Indian night.

In this 'Winged Dance' the Sun of Justice and the lame man he healed dance together, each on one leg as does Nataraj and those who join in the movement of the divine Dancer. Jesus too is 'Lord of the Dance', leading his followers, those healed by his joy-giving Spirit, in his dance of bliss - as the song at the end of this chapter celebrates. Healer and healed together share in the ecstatic playfulness of the new creation of God.

At our Bangalore college we expressed the dancing activity of Jesus in this way:

> (***Loka-pala*** and ***Bhakta-dipa***, meaning 'Lord of the World', and 'Light of your Lovers', are sung by all)
>
> *Source of all life, dancing in bliss:* ***Loka-pala***
> *Breaking down walls, making new space :* ***Bhakta-dipa***
>
> *Burning up wrong, creating afresh :* ***Loka-pala***
> *Calling the throng, follow in faith :* ***Bhakta-dipa***
>
> *Led by the Lord, power in his Name :* ***Loka-pala***
> *Healing by word, restoring the lame :* ***Bhakta-dipa***
>
> *Casting out powers, raising the dead:* ***Loka-pala***
> *Calming life's storms, removing all dread :* ***Bhakta-dipa***
>
> *Serving the poor, blessed from above :* ***Loka-pala***
> *Tested by fire, aflame with God's love :* ***Bhakta-dipa***
>
> *Seeking the lost, sharing our pain :* ***Loka-pala***
> *Love at such cost, rising again :* ***Bhakta-dipa***
>
> *Lighting our path, dancing ahead :* ***Loka-pala***
> *Leading through death, lifting to life :* ***Bhakta-dipa***

16 The Healing Tree

Our final story (found in Matthew 26-27, Mark 14-15, Luke 22-23) is one that would seem to be about anything but healing. There's betrayal, tears, bewilderment; there's despair, false witness, cowardice; there's jeering, there's opportunism, there's an unholy alliance; there's violence, sadism, agony. There's a nightmarish dream, there's painful lashing, stumbling with fatigue, a wounding spear-thrust. There's darkness at noon and the strange tearing of the temple veil. In fact there are a hundred stories woven into the one story, the long story of the passion and death of Jesus. But there's little sign of healing it would seem.

That's exactly what the watching crowds shouted at him in ridicule: 'Where's your healing power now? Physician, heal yourself. Come down from the cross if you really are the one to restore peace and right and wholeness to us!' But nothing seemed to happen; only those brief seven words from Jesus — words expressing his human need for a drink, as well as his human concern for his mother; words expressing his wild despair that God may have forsaken him, as well as his quiet conviction that all was well, all was now complete; words expressing his forgiveness of those who crucified him and his promise of paradise to a criminal condemned to die with him.

Yet, this horrifying death was seen by the Gospel writers as the climax of a healing life. This is how Peter summarised his life: 'He went around doing good and healing all. . . for God was with him. . Then they put him to death by hanging him on a tree.' (Acts 10:38) And in his Letter Peter makes an even clearer link between the death of Jesus and his healing work: 'Christ himself suffered for you and left you a pattern. . . He himself bore our sins in his body on the cross. . . It is by his wounds that you have been healed.' Indeed, it was not long before that wooden cross was being called a 'healing tree', the 'tree of life' that grows beside the 'river of the water of life', and whose 'leaves are for the healing of the nations' (Revelation 22:2). It was as though those originally dead cruciform beams had sprouted new shoots of living growth, and the cross became a 'power', potent to heal and bring hope and new life. What was previously a symbol of death had become a potent symbol of life.

This raises the important question of the power of symbols and images. East and West, far too many people underrate the power of imagery. In the East there is the concern to move beyond the 'mere name and form', which may well entail doing away altogether with the imagery that conditions our thinking and feeling. In the West the 'Enlightenment' led us to think that thinking is everything, the symbols that transcend rationality are nothing. Yet, in both East and West, increasingly it is the intrinsic message of images that is used to exploit the unwary. This is especially true of the world of consumer-advertising and in the media-world, where communications-skills are utilised for the control of people's minds. Images carry power, for they can be pregnant with hidden meaning.

In our religious community, our very identity, and our sense of how God is God, are embodied in the symbols through which faith is expressed. And no symbol is more central to Christian faith than the cross. No image is more potent than the crucified Jesus. It is, literally, *crucial* to our way of understanding God and of understanding life. No doubt the theories by which we have tried to explain the cross of Jesus have often been not only feeble, or far-fetched, they have sometimes been grotesque, making God in the image of some power-drunk nobleman, or devious merchant, or legalistic judge. And yet, the symbols endure, and we are compelled to go on trying to interpret, to draw out their meaning for our lives and for our faith.

What are we, then, to make of the image of the tree used, not only of the cross, but of Jesus himself? It's an image that is very deep-rooted in the Indian way of looking at things. The tree has been seen in India (as, of course, in older cultures almost everywhere) as epiphanic in both primal and classical life, and is still prominent in modern imagery. 'Asia's thinking is tree-shaped', claims Cecil Hargreaves in his *Asian Christian Thinking*. Tagore, for example, often pictures reality as a tree, following the lead of the widely popular Bhagavad Gita, where the Peepal Tree is endowed with cosmic proportions, its roots strangely reaching into the heavens

"LIFTED UP"

above and its branches deep into the earth below. So it is surprising that there hasn't been more reflection by Indian Christian theologians on Jesus as the tree of life. In general it is the theologically sensitive artists, such as Jyoti Sahi and Lucy D'Souza, who have linked cross and tree, and helped us reflect on the significance of Jesus as the tree of life.

Jyoti's 'Lifted Up' here shows the golden Bird, having come 'down to earth', now rising up through the branches of the tree of life. The tree too has a similar dual movement; the Banyan is famed for its roots reaching down from its upward-pointing branches. Thus heaven and earth touch each other at this point, where the healing Bird is caught by the tree, suffers on the tree; and by means of this tree of suffering draws earth and her children up to the heaven of God's new world.

Here we look at Jesus as the *healing tree*, though a tree that is planted firmly in the history of the cross, in his suffering and dying and rising, that act of ultimate healing for the world. For while ours may still be an archetypal tree, sharing features with the sacred tree of many cultures, it is also grounded in a very distinct history. So there is here in the tree of the cross of Jesus the confluence of two powerful story-streams, one the common stream of our human archetypal history, the other our peculiar Christian history. Both flow deep in our consciousness and faith.

I

First, then, let us look at the *tree as a focus for healing*. A sacred tree features both at the beginning of the Bible (Genesis 2 and 3) and in its last chapter (Revelation 22). In one the tree of life is at the centre of the garden, the place given for human habitation. In the other the tree of life is at the centre of the heavenly city — here the eternal place God has prepared for the redeemed community. Both are watered by a life-giving stream. In the Garden of Eden there was in fact another tree, the tree of knowledge. Against God's command,

Eve, and then Adam, ate the fruit of this tree and thus gained an awareness of themselves, a self-consciousness, that estranged them from God. They were no longer innocents in paradise. And even the fruit of the tree of knowledge was taken away because of this estrangement.

Estrangement is a strong motif in the Old Testament. Of the many references to trees, the majority by far speak of the cutting down of trees, of their being despoiled and dead. The same is the case with the *hand* of God. There are many more references to the hand of God being stretched out in anger because of the estranged state of humans, than for healing and blessing.

But there is a similar ambiguity in the Buddhist tradition. The tree of enlightenment, the Bodhi or Peepal Tree, is a central image for Buddhists. Yet, there are also many references to the need to 'uproot' the tree that is the 'sap of life', the symbol of desire. And in many other religions too, before any renewal there has to be renunciation, 'repentance'. Before rebirth there has to be a breaking with the past, a radical uprooting of that which now conditions our being, opening up the way for healing.

The tree, therefore, is often as much an image of the *need for healing* as for healing itself. Probably such 'tension' is found in all faiths in one form or another. The innocent state of Eden has been lost everywhere, and we should not romanticise human experience in any cultural tradition. Even so, it is a fact of human cultural experience especially in the life of forest tribal people that the tree is venerated as a potent symbol of life, of fruitfulness, of good, of healing. And this primal vision of the tree as carrying healing power has permeated all Indian cultural tradition. It is often felt that by their very existence certain trees exude a healing aura. But is not this what every good environmentalist should affirm: human health, the whole planet's health, depends upon the existence of a sufficient area of forest.

As the statement on the New Internationalist cardigan I like to wear says: 'A Tree is for Life'. And this runs counter to so much that our modern civilisation stands for. 'A tree is for chopping, for burning, for pulping, for producing some other commodity.' That, generally, would be more true to contemporary life.

At this point the Chipko movement among the Hill People, especially the women, in the south-western part of the Himalayan region in India is an outstanding sign for our times. Its origins were actually in Rajasthan, where the women of the Bishnoi people defied their local Rajah and his men, and risked death by hugging their trees, sacred and central to their very identity, rather than allow these trees to be cut down. Over a hundred women were said to have been killed in that act of confrontation.

This is the story that the women of the Chipko movement have taken as their starting point. They too are 'tree-huggers'; hence the term 'Chip-ko'. For them the 'sacredness' of their trees lies in their life-providing benefits — the fruit, the fodder for cattle, the fuel for cooking, shade from the sun, protection and fertiliser for the soil. But as essential as any is the gift of healing — through roots, bark, resin and leaves. For them, a tree is for wholeness of life and for healing.

And so we are reminded of the final chapter in Revelation, as the biblical story comes full circle through the healing acts of Jesus, culminating in his sacrificial death: He is 'the tree of life. . . . whose leaves are for the healing of the nations.'

From time to time in our college at Bangalore we celebrated a liturgy of 'Sharing Earth's Life', one of services we brought out in *Worship in an Indian Context*. Part of this liturgy is my '*Ballad of Creation'*, to be danced as well as sung. Here are stanzas 3 and 4:

Then God, rejoicing with all earth,
In dance more worlds created;
God's bliss brought countless stars to birth,
God's fulness undepleted.
Now join this cosmic dance of bliss,
Step gladly, for the rhythm's his.
All earthlings in one life must share;
All bound as one in mutual care;
Drawn by the drum-beat of God's love,
We in God's dance so freely move;

For all that lives is God's.
Our great Creator, we recall,
On earth a tree once planted;
A tree of life, whose leaves would heal
The ills of all, was granted.
A tree whose arms outstretched above
Though humans, plundering its fruit,
Fell from their innocent estate,
Hope now lies in this cross-shaped tree,
And blood-red blossoms point the way
To life again, to glory;
To life again, to glory.

Jesus is the healing tree. Charles Wesley is but one of many hymn-writers that use this image when depicting the cross:

Endless scenes of wonder rise
From that mysterious tree.

Elsewhere Wesley speaks of 'the wounds which all my sorrows heal'. Much earlier, in the sixth century, Fortunatus wrote hymns that refer again and again to the 'tree of death' that is also the 'tree of life':

. . . . *Inviting all the world to see:*
Our God has suffered on the tree!
O tree, most beautiful, most glad,
O tree in royal purple clad,
Chosen from noble stock to bear
The holy limbs that suffer there. . . .
Whom by the cross though dost restore,
Preserve and govern evermore.

Clearly, then, in Christian faith there is a long history of devotion to the cross as 'the healing tree', restoring wholeness to human life, just as the tree is in God's created world a source of healing and well-being.

II (a)

Secondly, though, we need to look more closely at *what kind of healing this cross-tree effects*. Three themes emerge most prominently in Christian faith in the cross. The first relates to the *atonement of humans estranged from God, the creation of a new relationship between human life and God's life*. At times this has been seen in terms of the need for a change in the attitude of *God*, as though it is *God's heart* that is estranged, *God's wrath* that needs pacifying. And because the offering of Jesus is perfect, it is said, God overlooks the sins of all others who believe in that Jesus as the atoning sacrifice. But this interpretation of the cross is ludicrously far removed from all that the many healing acts of Jesus tell us of his mind and of the mind of God.

Yet, there *is* this fundamental need for at-one-ment. We are in need of a new kind of relationship with God. Much creation spirituality, certainly much New Age thinking, just ignores this dimension of our being altogether. Of course we should stress the wonder of 'original blessing', as Matthew Fox does. But, even a casual look at the history of the human race, with all its cruelty, its violence, its oppression, and no one can miss the reality of how we are as humans. We are so very far from what we should be and could be. We are radically, at our very *roots,* out of tune with the good, the true, the right, the just. In the Apostle's words: 'We have all sinned and fallen short of the glory of God.' Christian faith has always affirmed that it is because somehow in our inmost being, in our heart and soul, we are estranged from God, the Root and Spring of all that is good and true and right and just, because we are estranged from Love, that we are flawed in the depth of our being in this fundamental way. We have 'fallen short of glory', and we are in need of at-one-ment with the Root of glory.

And by recalling the story of Jesus' dramatic, self-denying act of death and rising to new life, and by sharing in that 'drama of salvation/healing', countless people have found it possible to break with their past and enter into a new sense of at-one-ment with God. This sense of new 'rootage' makes so much else possible, even if in itself the cross is not everything, as Christians from Paul onwards have been prone to claim. But it is certainly a basis for new life. *Potentially*, yes, everything is renewed when heart and mind share in the dying and rising of the 'tree of life'.

Jesus himself uses this tree-imagery in speaking of the vine and its branches. To be 'fruitful' in their lives and actions, those with love for him and faith in him are to 'remain' in him just like the branches of a tree. Mutual in-dwelling is the key to growth and fruitfulness (John 15). And such life-changing companionship — which literally means 'sharing-of-bread-together' — such renewing friendship is possible, says Jesus, because he 'lays down his life for his friends'. This is what makes a new at-one-ment possible for those who believe him to be their healing tree. As the Apostle put it: 'God was in Christ, making enemies into his friends' (or as the earlier English put it: 'Reconciling the world to himself'. 2 Corinthians 5:19). Or we might say, 'Healing the rift'.

II (b)

Then there is a *second* theme that emerges in connection with the passion and death of Jesus: *estranged people find they are in a new relationship with each other*. What was the apostolic word, referring to what was then seen as the most fundamental of all divisions in human community, that dividing 'God's people, Israel', and all other Goyim, or Gentile people, people 'without hope and without God'? 'You that used to be far off have been brought close, by the blood of Christ. For he is the peace between us, and has made the two into one. . . His purpose was, by restoring peace, to create a single New Man. . . and through the cross to reconcile both to God in one body' (Ephesians 2:14-16). What the Epistle affirms here of the rift between just two human communities can obviously be applied to the estrangement between *any* human communities. The passion and death of Jesus has provided the basis for a new kind of human community. The age-old wounds, the painful scars resulting from long and tragic enmity, *can* be healed. A new global community *is* possible.

The only 'globalisation' we know at present, though, is a far cry from this vision of human togetherness, God's intent that there be 'one body', 'one new humanity'. The bonds that grow between us at present are merely the tentacles of commercial greed stretching out to gain control over as many local economies as possible. It is this trans-national economic colonising that then provides the framework for the westernising of local cultural life. Even Christian world mission has so often been a kind of ecclesiastical colonising. The dynamics of local community life have been ignored, and the cultural values of the missioning community have been taken as God-given and absolute.

The pattern of dying together to all that excludes the other, of rising together to new life that accepts and uplifts the other — in other words, sharing in this cross-shaped way of Jesus — is the way by which the wounds of our community life can be healed. Is it not by now abundantly clear that there will be no healing of the tragically painful wounds our mutual enmities have inflicted on human life in Bosnia, in Northern Ireland, in Sri Lanka, in Kashmir, in Assam, and in many other places in God's world, unless there is a radical dying together to those ego-boosting elements in our past that have kept us separate?

Jesus speaks of life in God's new world as being like the life of a great tree, grown up from such small beginnings. It is a globally inclusive tree, providing habitat and resources for all the peoples of the world. For 'people will come from east and west, from north and south, and will sit down to feast. . . Then those who are now last will be first, and those who are now first will be last' (Luke 13:19, 29-30). This is the kind of upside-down consequence for our human togetherness of taking the tree of death as a tree of life.

II (c)

And finally, a *third* theme that emerges in connection with a tree that means at-one-ment is the *uplifting of earth's life to a new status*. In the past, it must be confessed, earth has not seemed to benefit from Christian reflection on the meaning of the cross. It is as though the thought of the lifeless, naked body of the crucified Jesus has led many of his followers to think of the body of earth as equally without life, as needing to be made naked and treeless, as needing to return to its pre-created state as 'a desolate void'.

But it is not his dead body that Jesus' followers are to meditate on; it is his resurrected body. When Jesus says, 'This is my body', and those who follow him take the bread through which he offers us a share in the life of that body, it is the earth-transfiguring, earth-resurrecting body that we are to reflect on.

But we have been part of a process that has almost mortally wounded the body of earth that it was God's purpose we should help to transfigure. I recall a story from the South Sea Islands told in a collection by Rita Snowden that I read in my youth. When their children ask, 'Why is there dew on the grass in the mornings?', the story is told of the time long ago when heaven and earth were united together, just like lovers of one heart and mind, one body. Then there came the great rift, and heaven and earth became separated. But each morning, earth weeps tears of sorrow as she remembers the one who loved her; she longs for that lost togetherness.

The Apostle too speaks of earth's longing; she 'awaits eagerly. . . the same glorious freedom as the children of God'. Until now in the whole of creation there are the tears and groans of childbirth, as we long for 'our bodies to be set free'. All creation is expectant with this hope of final healing (Romans 8:19-23). And in the risen body of Jesus, affirm his followers, we see the green budding of spring, the 'first-fruits', of a renewed and whole creation.

The risen Jesus of the cross is the tree in which earth and heaven are linked again, lovers again, and the great rift is healed. With roots reaching deep into earth's inner life, and with branches stretching high into heaven, this tree of life is a cosmic meeting-point, a healing-point for earth's body and for those who now give themselves to following the way of Jesus the healer.

Epilogue:

Restoring the Wounded Psyche of a would-be Guru

It is our own stories that determine which stories of others mean most to us. So I am now, by way of conclusion, going to take something of a risk and recount a very personal healing story of my own. The risk is that others may find this somewhat self-indulgent on my part. But it was this episode that opened up the healing ministry of Jesus for me. For much of my life these healing stories about Jesus, though valued, were hardly central to faith. It was not here that I saw the crucial clues for understanding the world and my own place in it.

Around ten years ago I found my inner world beginning to disintegrate. By the end of 1988 I was diagnosed as being in a state of severe Depression. I often feel we should use a different term for this condition; for it bears scant resemblance to those periods of feeling a little low in spirit, being 'a bit depressed', that we all go through now and then. And because the term is the same, when it is said that so-and-so has Depression, because also there's little external evidence to show for it, most people's response is to say, or at least feel: 'She needs to pull herself together. Don't we all get depressed at times?'

Clinical Depression, as the medical people diagnosed my condition, relates to feeling 'a bit depressed' in the way a ravenously marauding tiger-shark relates to a gentle goldfish cruising harmlessly in a little bowl in your front-room. Even though symptoms may differ from person to person, those who have been in the grip of the trauma of Depression will invariably say the same thing: 'I would not have believed the mind could cause such pain, that life could be so much like a continual and quite terrifying nightmare. I would not have believed my feelings could be so much out of control, or that we could feel so much misery, day after day, often night after night.'

Let me very briefly describe how my own Depression developed. Several factors contributed. There was the stress of persistent overwork. In the Bangalore college where I worked for several years, I ended up actually doing about three jobs in one. Clearly this is not the place to begin listing all my duties during that seven or eight-year period before fatigue set in. Suffice it to say that for most of that period I was working, often at a quite intense level, for an average of well over 100 hours a week. Much of it was great adrenalin-pumping stuff. Teaching about the wonderfully diverse, always fascinating religions of India to theological students who have to come to terms with the multi-cultural ferment that is India today, was bound to be exciting. Then there were endless writing projects, and challenging engagements in that multi-cultural context. Of course not all was exciting work. For I'd been loaded with several routine chores, about which I'd felt unable to say 'no'. I was aware, but not assertive enough to do anything about it, that 'a willing horse eventually becomes a dead donkey'!

It was in fact the exciting engagements that also proved to be a stress-factor. On the one hand there was probably far too much ego-stimulation for the health of my soul in much that I was doing. One day I might be invited to give a lecture to a large group of Hindu scholars on some aspect of their own Vaishnava tradition. The next day there might be the task of engaging on inter-faith issues with a visiting professor from perhaps Harvard or Oxford, for Bangalore seemed to be an essential port of call for all manner of eminent scholars from East and West. Soon after there might be a paper to be read at an all-India seminar on ecology and the need for an eco-cultural faith, on which I'd developed some new ideas several years before eco-theology became fashionable. All this — and much more — I fear was probably nurturing a good crop of over-inflated, self-deluding hubris. And as everyone knows, 'Pride comes before a fall'.

It is within myself, then, that I recognise at least some of the root-causes of the breakdown later. On the other hand, there were also external stress-factors. Most of my colleagues were thoroughly supportive and helpful. Just one or two key people, whose encouragement I needed, either did not approve of anyone moving out into the sort of frontier theology I was increasingly engaged in; or resented the fact that here was a non-Indian taking a lead in, for example, inter-cultural worship, or in other forms of contextual engagement, when really he should leave it to nationals. Is this not just a new expression of the imperialist spirit? And I certainly do not blame any Indian national for feeling this way, in view of our post-colonial context.

Then there were one or two who were critical of the particular form my inter-cultural engagement took. Here we need to note the emergence of a liberationist theological perspective that vigorously rejects any over-valuing of the so-called 'Great Traditions' in India's cultural history; and it was within a 'Great Tradition' that much of my research and experience happened to be.

I must not give a false impression here though. From my earliest days in India I had formed close friendships with people coming from the so-called 'untouchable' communities. They have now come to identify themselves as 'Dalits', the 'broken ones'. My first pastoral Guide, my Bishop (still greatly loved), my colleagues, my Telugu language teacher, were almost all Dalit. I felt a strong sense of identity with them. And yet, I also came increasingly to see the immense value, the richness, of the so-called 'Brahmanic' traditions, especially the *Bhakti* traditions, both in Sanskrit and the vernacular languages, which have made such a great impact on Indian cultural and religious life. Obviously there were plenty of raw materials here for the development of a vigorous tension within myself!

Gradually during my thirty years in India, however, quite apart from any inherent tension within my own experience, a divisive polarising of these two streams of Indian cultural life developed within theological circles. Many Dalit leaders have now come to see all Sanskritic, indeed all Hindu, traditions as wholly oppressive. Brahmanic culture *has*, it is true, been oppressive in many and sometimes quite cruel ways. Yet, everything in me longs to find ways somehow of drawing out the inter-connectedness, of reconciling, not rejecting wholesale, these tensive streams within India's cultural and ethnic diversity.

And this leads into a third stress-factor: I have to confess my life-long personal difficulty in coping with confrontation. It's not that I am unable to confront those I believe to be wrong. At times duty has led to my having to do this with some vigour. But I find it very difficult; there is in my psyche an excessive need for the approval of others. And there are no doubt childhood traumas to which this can be traced, though this is not the place to attempt to delve into such early experience.

Another cause of stress was something quite different. Eventually it was discovered, following a liver biopsy, that I'd been suffering for some time from a non-acute form of 'chronic persistent hepatitis'. Up till then it had been assumed that all my symptoms — lack of energy, digestive problems, headaches, dizziness, and so on — were the result of stress, all part of the Depression. And who can say which was causing which, the mind-body interdependence being so subtle. I must say, though, that it was something of a relief to find out that there was a very specific *physical* problem, no matter how it was connected to the mental illness.

And then there was the move from India, in 1988. At this time there was still not much to be greatly alarmed about, though in my de-briefing medical it was said that I was already in some degree of Depression, and should consult my GP. Here it should be made very clear that I did not want to leave India. In fact I found it a devastating prospect; the future looked like an endless night. I tried hard to convince myself that it was the *right* move, and therefore God's leading. There were the needs of my family to think of — there were elderly parents and the need of a home-base for our children around the age of twenty. And, of course, my health had been deteriorating. My weight, for example, was down by 40%, leaving me looking like bones in a skin-bag. And I was not sleeping well.

All this self-persuasion, however, could not lessen a deep sense of *desolation*, of *bereavement*, on leaving the country, the place, the people, I had come to love so much; the context that I had become so locked into, so dependent on for my sense of identity and self-fulfilment.

But the most vicious symptoms were still to come. Within a few weeks of leaving India, I was working in Leicester, having taken over my friend Martin Forward's inner city work. This involved pastoral work with two middle-sized congregations, one of them in the 'notorious' Highfields area of the city. With 50% of the members coming from a Caribbean background — people of whom I had no previous experience — and most other members being White, this was a challenge in itself. And attached to this second church was a high-profile Community Project, with around a dozen different organisations —Day Centre for those recovering from mental illness, Breakfast and Supper for the homeless a needy, Advice Centre for Asian people, Interfaith programmes, Youth Groups, Playgroup, Elderly Infirm Group, and so on. Most of the workers were paid by Leicester City Council, but overall management was chaired, and was therefore the responsibility of, the minister. That was me.

And it all terrified me, as much as anything because in my 55 years I'd had no experience at all of that sort of work — apart from the inter-cultural connection. Even that, though, proved to be so very different from how things were in India. I had also had virtually no previous pastoral work of the kind called for in this situation. I knew almost nothing of how Methodism worked. For most of my ministering life my first task had been teaching college students in a far-off continent. And we were so thoroughly ecumenical that students and staff ranged from Syrian Orthodox and Catholic to Salvation Army and Seventh Day Adventist. With the Caribbean people of Leicester at first I felt very hesitant; I had just not known them before. But at least on that front I grew in confidence, and within the first year I'd come to love them greatly. And indeed people generally were very kind and uncritical, in spite of what must surely have been an obvious diffidence and lack of experience.

No amount of kindliness, however, could curtail the growth of this monster within my psyche. There was a debilitating lack of self-confidence, preventing me from doing anything new, anything pioneering, in the way I'd delighted in in the past. I was simply afraid that people would find the unexpected unacceptable. In fact creativity dried up completely, my mind just ceasing to function with the flexibility I'd found so exciting in my Bangalore days.

Even the simplest concentration was a serious problem. While talking with people I was visiting, immense effort was required merely to listen to what they were saying. My mind was for ever intent on escaping somewhere else, even when with people I wanted to be because they were so welcoming and I wanted to minister well to them. Add to this an increasing inability to remember even the simplest facts, including people's names, whether they were single or married, had children or not — all the things a pastor must remember, and it can be imagined what confusion there was in my mind when it came to the more complex and often difficult matters arising in the weekly Project Team meetings, and the monthly meetings of the Management Committee over which I had to preside.

Here, though, as in church business meetings, there was invariably the very competent guidance of our lay treasurer. He and other key-figures, were always supportive, even when it must have been only too clear that I was out of my depth and floundering. One of these supporters was herself suffering from painful cancer, from which she died not long after I left. It was my first experience of ministering constantly to the sick, the dying and the bereaved. While such ministry is in itself greatly draining for those who tend to relate closely to people, it is also strangely uplifting at times. Helpful, unstinting support came, too, from my predecessor, Martin, which is as unusual in ministerial circles as in secular life; rivalry and jealousy run deep in the human heart. So Martin's friendship meant much, even if a sense of abysmal failure darkened my every thought. Also able to lift the spirit a little were the monthly times of get-together of the four neighbouring inner-city clergy, Anglican, Catholic and Moravian. We even did a very successful service together, broadcast nationally.

But these various sources of support did not prevent attacks of sheer panic from becoming increasingly strong. Anxiety, despair, disorientation was there all the time. On the last of these, for example, I could not drive or walk more than one street away from our home without taking a street map with me, or I would be lost completely. As to the despair — as I walked the streets, I was sure everyone could see quite clearly the torment and disintegration that was there inside me. Surely it was written plainly on my face, for all my attempts to smile with pastoral cheerfulness at people as we passed. The panic attacks, though, were worse than this continual gnawing despair. Panic began to pounce most fiercely at around 3.00 in the morning. I would wake suddenly with this immediate and desperate sense that everything is completely out of control;

that I am utterly incapable of coping with the responsibilities that have been placed on me; that total disaster surely awaits me there in the future. Sometimes I would be shaking in an agony of fear. Occasionally I would have to wake my wife for fear that either I was about to go entirely insane, or that I might try to end all this pain by doing away with my own life. In fact there was not a day when the thought of suicide did not come to mind, however strongly I thrust it away. Once there was such sudden pressure around my chest and extreme difficulty of breathing that I felt it must be a heart attack. Of course it was not. My wife was wonderfully supportive, though working hard herself as a teacher in one of the inner city schools. She had to put up with a lot of tears, as well as the long silences, on my part. How anyone faces Depression alone I just cannot imagine.

I even began to look back on my life — of teaching, writing, enabling faith, ministering to 'untouchable' people, administering aid to the needy, all the inter-cultural efforts, all the engagement with 'people of other faiths'—it all seemed quite worthless, because I myself lacked any worth. Everything I did, part of me would see as flawed and useless. I increasingly lost any sense of clear self-identity. I was a nobody, however much I may still be acting as though I was somebody.

Looking back at the notes of my sermons during that two or three-year period, remarkably they seem quite presentable. I certainly struggled hard to communicate in words and with ideas and images that would mean something to the very different sort of people I was now communicating faith to.

Yet, before and after each sermon, part of me would say, 'You are so inept at this, you are such a worthless minister, how can you imagine that your words will mean anything to these people?' Sometimes my wife would have to virtually push me out of the manse door to get me to the church. And I recall that I could never look directly at people as I was speaking. I was forced to look over their heads, or towards them in a general way, but never look them directly in the eye. It was a lack of contact I'd never known in the past, even when struggling in the early India years to preach in Telugu. And I was afraid to stand up without every word carefully prepared.

Even if *what* I said was good enough, there was, I'm sure, a heavily laboured quality to my preaching during that period. My vain attempts to infuse life and vigour into my delivery must, I'm sure, have seemed like the final frantic desperation of one who knows he is doomed.

Lying behind all this was another deeper anxiety. Was I not supposed to be THE MINISTER? Had I not been for years regarded as a sort of GURU to many generations of Indian students? That's how many of them actually addressed me, 'Guru'. Was I not to be a healer to people, rather than one now so desperately in need of healing? Was I not supposed to lead people to wholeness of being, rather than be so fearfully fractured within? Was I not to be a source of joy to others, rather than a soul eaten up with misery? Was I not an utter fraud, masquerading as the Minister, but in reality no more than a squeaking mouse?

Strange as it may seem, there does not appear to have been any serious crisis of my faith in God. Within a few months of entering this period of mental crisis I was sent to see a psychiatrist. I had only been telling my story as best I could for a few minutes when he seized on the trauma of the transition I'd made from India, and the work there, to England, and the work here. He also wondered if there was a crisis of faith; and I had to give an account of what I still believed in spite of such belief being put on the rack. As it happens, he declared himself to be an atheist, so I had to work hard at putting my faith as convincingly and rationally as possible.

For a while he tried cognitive therapy — trying to get me to re-pattern my way of looking at things. But the misery increased, and we had to move on to anti-depressant drugs. As the psychiatrist explained, my Depression was not just a matter of my mind and feelings being a bit out of control. When you're in a depressed condition, your brain begins pumping out chemicals that upset the whole equilibrium of your body. That's why the anti-depressant drugs become necessary — to act as a buffer to cut off this chemical output. But they are, as he put it cheerfully, very toxic, and you'll have to suffer for a while by taking as high a dose as your system will cope with, and for a good long period. All the evidence shows that the more you take and the longer the period, the better the results eventually. But, meanwhile, you have to suffer, even if it is in a different way from what you're suffering now.

In other words, anti-depressants often have side-effects. Well, they certainly did with me. The worst side-effect was the shakes; my hands were so shaky when offering bread and wine in the Eucharist, that even there I was not allowed to forget that I'm a useless nobody. There was also the constant lack of saliva in the mouth, the inability to urinate, the constipation, the rapid increase in weight, greater dizziness and pressure in the head than before, the quaver in the voice I used to think of as nicely resonant, and so on. But—those little pills did quell the panic, and did enable me to sleep fairly well.

Medication was not my only means of healing. I've already mentioned the unwavering support of my wife, and the encouragement of church members, especially when I *told* them something of my inner torment. Some degree of openness was, I felt, healthier than the usual professional secrecy about such things. A particular form of encouragement from my psychiatrist is also worth mentioning. I had told him a little of my past, and of my writing. A few days later, while in Oxford, he went to Blackwells and asked if they had anything of mine. It seems they had at least one — *Vision, Tradition, Interpretation,* dealing with the nature of religion, the study of traditions, and especially with how the theological process (in any religion) fits into this. Published in Germany, it is very costly. Even so, he bought a copy — being, he said, very interested in what I had to say about a phenomenological approach to religion. That one concrete act of buying what I had written probably did more for me than any of the words he spoke to help restore my shattered self-confidence.

And what other, more specific, ways of healing were there? At one of my churches there was a healing group. We decided to hold a monthly Healing Communion as a central part of the group's programme. I composed a short order for this (included later in Howard Booth's *Seven Whole Days*) which we tried out together and found embodied effectively our faith in the healing work of God-in-Christ. At these services each month I spoke in turn about all the healing acts of Jesus. This preaching was very brief and intimate, but I drew out as forcefully as I could the meaning for us and our need that these healing stories of Jesus offered. The sixteen chapters of this book are fleshed-out forms of those short talks. The healing eucharist was the one place where I could still really engage with people in my preaching, look them in the eye.

During the eucharist others would place their hands on those requesting healing. There was hardly a month when I did not ask for healing myself — and receive it. For one thing there was the very tangible heat generated in my body by the hands placed on me. The very least effect of this was a comforting, relaxing sense of inner warmth. By its attitude of encouragement and support, providing an atmosphere where I was (even if only for a short time) able to feel relaxed, that healing group played an important role in the healing process.

My reflecting on the Jesus stories, in preparation for and during the Communion, was an equally important part of this healing work; this was further confirmed first by the taking of the healing gifts of body and blood, his whole being, that the Risen Lord offers us; and then by the healing he offers through those who place their hands on the sick in the faith that this Risen One is still at work. The wounds in my psyche were very deep indeed; the scars were painful for a long time; but gradually healing did take place.

There were, of course, other means to effecting this restoring of wholeness. I'll mention just four more. One could be seen as no more than a regular pastoral duty — visiting the homes of those who looked to me as 'the minister'. Some visits were less 'healing' to my spirit than others of course. In general, though — presumably because it helped build a sense of continuity with my overseas' past — I found my visits especially to the numerous Caribbean members strangely uplifting. The majority had come to England from Antigua many years earlier, and had been exposed at different times to all manner of racist abuse. And yet there was so evident in many of them an inner strength, a buoyancy of spirit, and a constancy of faith, that again and again seemed to lighten my own darkened spirit.

Another means of healing was the art of Jyoti Sahi, to whom I've referred several times in the course of these essays. Jyoti is an Indian artist, a Catholic, who seeks to express his vision of the world - with all its pain and its promise of glory — by drawing on imagery both from his Christian and his Indian traditions. In exploring both these streams that flow into his own selfhood he increasingly draws on the primal elements found in them, especially the stories and images of India's tribal people. Jyoti, and his wife Jane, have been close friends of my wife and myself for around 20 years, for they live close to Bangalore where we were teaching for a long time. As part of my sabbatical in late 1990, we went to stay with Jyoti and Jane at their village *ashram*, where Jane also has a school for local children. I was already beginning to recover, but in the weeks just prior to the sabbatical my father had died, and my wife had undergone surgery for breast cancer. The weeks we were able to spend quietly back in that Indian 'place of refuge' meant that there was no relapse, but a hastening of the healing — for both of us.

And even in the long two years since I had left India, three woodcuts of Jyoti's, done many years before on key themes in the Psalms, hung above my bed. One is of a man curled in a foetal position, head on bony knees, hands clasped over crossed ankles, eyes closed in desperate resignation. He is held in the safe waters of the womb, waters that flow as tears from the all-seeing eye of God, a watchful eye that weeps with an all-encompassing compassion. I looked at that picture, and other pictures of Jyoti's, every day, and sometimes at night when I did not sleep. They too — images of God's painful caring — helped in the healing.

A third means of healing came through those times when we were able to escape to the wilderness places we love so much. Even in early childhood I had felt an almost mystical sense of affinity with nature in the quiet boggy glades of the valley running through the family farm in Devon. In India it had been the same: in the forests, for example, of the area of Andhra where we had been asked to build and then supervise a hostel for children of the forest hills; camping with the family in the beautiful valley by the river Kaveri some 50 miles from Bangalore; trekking in the hills and forests of Nepal, from the home of our friends Finlay and Rachel, Hodge engaged in agricultural and development work there; and all this focused in our love of birds and my obsession with bird-photography. A sure way of recovering some degree of mental poise and peace, during those years of Depression, was to turn my mind to one or other of these wilderness scenes. Nearly every night, one or other of these scenes, or images of outstanding birds, were deliberately brought to mind. After returning from India, there were almost annual trips to the wild places of Scotland, and a month of my sabbatical in the wonderfully impressive open spaces of New South Wales, with more friends from our Indian story, Nola and Geoff, Oddie teaching South Asian history at Sydney University. During those dark years these visits too served to open up, even if for a time, windows of light within me, and helped in the healing.

The fourth means of healing is not really one among others; it is one that seemed to undergird all the others and give them meaning and power. I refer to my repeating of the Name. I remember each morning when I walked to my friend Adam Ali's corner shop for the milk and daily paper, each step I took on the pavement was accompanied by the rhythmic inner repeating of the syllable of one of the names of Jesus. JE-SUS MY LORD; JE-SUS MY LIFE; LIGHT OF THE WORLD; MY BROTHER, MY FRIEND; MY HEALTH, MY PEACE; ANASTASIS; and many more. Four syllables were fitted into each in-breathing and each out-breathing. In effect it was a modified yogic exercise, though it also fitted in with exercises another friend, who practises hypno-therapy, had given me. Was it significant that, when attempts were made to hypnotise me, I never actually 'went under'? Nothing could relax me that much. However, the self-relaxing exercises my friend gave did prove helpful, and still do.

It was the Consultant who had found the hepatitis who eventually suggested — after another year of toxic medication for that condition — that it would be sensible to retire from the demanding full-time work I was doing, and work whenever I felt able. This was four years before I was due to retire. And it has proved a further liberating move, even though it meant accepting my fragility, accepting that I no longer had the resources to cope with work in which there's much responsibility for organising things. So a major period of my life was over. Yet it was a move that not only set me free from stress-sources, it set me free for a life-style, for activities, that further strengthen the healing process — a great deal of writing, that I'd so feared was gone for ever; bird-watching and bird-photography; visits back to India, to see old friends, to do a certain amount of teaching and lecturing; the occasional preaching and leading congregations in worship. The healing hand of Jesus still reaches out to touch those who share his vision of a restored world, of a new future for the human family, of wholeness for all God's creation.

Name/Subject Index

Adam 124, 125, 156
Aggiornamento 27
Agitation 14, 22
Alien(ated) 41-42, 49-50, 87-93
Alternative medicine 4
Amazement 29, 30, 56
Ambiguity 111-112
Andhra Pradesh 8, 9, 103
Anger (of Jesus) 42-44
Anglican 70, 168
Apostle, apostolic 1, 19, 89, 142-146, 159
Appasamy, Bishop 123
Aramaic 96, 100
Aum 73
Aurobindo 24
Azariah, Bishop 54

Bacon, Francis 124
Ballad of Creation 157
Bangalore 1, 151, 157, 164, 167, 173
Bartimaeus 78-86
Beautiful Gate 141, 143, 148
Bethesda, Bethany 1, 57, 103, 132, 134
Bhagavad Gita 144, 154
Bhakta (i) 19, 24, 135, 146, 152, 165
Bird, Bird-imagery ii, 43, 55, 63, 73, 90, 98, 120, 155
Black (people) 44, 45, 140
Blind(ness), Blind beggar 78-86, 115, 121-131
Body iii, 1,4, 17, 19, 20, 25 (and passim)
Booth, H 171
Bosnia 72, 92, 161
Buddha 2, 13, 26, 156

Canaan(ite) 88, 89
Capernaum 22, 31
Carer 69
Caribbean 166-167, 172
Catholic 70, 129, 147, 167, 168, 173

Index

Centurion (Roman Officer) 31-37
Child(ren) i 45, 56-66, 110
Chipko 157
Chopra, Deepak 128
Christology 7
Compassion 32
Conflict 50, 89, 117-119
Confusion 56-60, 111-112
Consumerism 15
Creation, Creator 24, 43, 86, 88-89, 96, 125, 150-151, 162
Creation-centred 4
Crippled 102-109
Cross, Crucifixion 24, 119, 153-162

Dalit 2, 44, 45, 46, 72, 80, 165
Dance, dancing 23, 150-152, 157
Darshana 126
Daughter 56-66, 88-93
Davies, S. 1
Deaf (-mute) 94-101
Death 19, 35, 55, 64-66, 119, 134-140, 168
Decapolis (Ten Towns) 47, 94-96
Demon(iac), Devil 11, 12, 14, 47-55, 87-89
Depression 19, 25, 42, 163-175
Descent (Avatara) 24
Deus absconditus 90
Dichpalli 39
Dickens 32, 34
Disciple 12-14, 49, 61 (and passim)
Domestics 32, 59
Donne, J. 106
Dornakal 45, 54
Drama(tic)2, 10, 22-23, 24, 27, 30, 90, 150, 159
D'Souza, Lucy 155

Eagle ii, iii, 139
Earth 4-5, 73-76, 100, 124, 157, 161-162
Ecological, Eco-habitat 2, 73, 164
Ecstatic 1
Ephphatha 94-101

Epileptic 18, 19, 64, 95, 110-120
Erukala 54
Estrangement 156, 159, 160
Eucharist 35, 172
Evangelical(s) 70, 82
Eve 156
Evil 88-89, 114, 130-131

Faith - passim
Family 29, 36, 69, 97-99, 134-136
Feminist 2, 17, 68, 75
Fever 11, 13-15, 18
Food 62-63, 135
Forgive(ness) 21, 24-27, 28,29
Fortunatus 158
Forward Martin 166, 168
Fox, Matthew 159
Freud 51
Fundamentalism 3, 7

Galilee 14, 49, 54, 94
Ganapati 151
Gandhi, Mahatma 53
Garasene, Gadarene 47, 57
Gentile 31, 87, 160
Gethsemene iii
Global(isation) 15, 26, 62, 71, 147, 160-161
Godavari 40, 49, 52, 104
Golden (bird,egg) 120
Gospel(s) iii, 1, 2, 3, 6, 27, 32, 35 (and passim)
Guru(s) 26, 71, 85, 92, 105, 128, 146, 163, 170

Hamsa (Swan) ii, 8, 15-16, 63, 73, 98, 139
Hand 15-17, 45, 56, 119, 150
Hanuman 8
Hargreaves, Cecil 154
Healing (group) 5, 16, 64, 171
Healing - passim
Heart (of God) 29, 159

Hindu(ism) 26
Hodge F and R 173
Home 16, 30, 55
Human(ness) 7, 13, 14, 32, 34, 60-61, 65, 96-97, 139
Humility 34-36
Humour (of Jesus) 12

Iconoclast 13
Impurity 70, 95
Indigenous 97
Injustice 32
Interconnected(ness) 19, 73-74, 165-66
Interfaith (Other faith) 33, 34, 164
Islam(ic) 91
Israel(ites) 31, 32

Jain(ism) 26
Jairus 19, 56-66
James 11, 56
Jerusalem 1, 79, 102, 132
Jesus - passim
Jiva-ahimsa 53
John 11, 56, 141, 143
Justice i, 5, 7, 84
Jyoti (Sahi) i, ii, 11, 10, 15-16, 23, 37, 43, 45, 55, 63, 73, 85, 90, 98, 107, 120 129, 139, 151, 155, 172-173.

Kakar, Sudhir 2
Karma 26, 41
King, Martin Luther 53
Kingdom (of God) iii, 44
Krishna 144, 146, 151

Lazarus 132-140
Leicester 50, 64, 166-167
Leprosy (Leper) 22, 38,-46

Liberation(ist) 4, 24, 29, 37, 165
Light 7, 85, 111, 121-131
Little Brothers 16
Listen 146-148
Locating (Jesus) 23
Look 38, 143-145
Luther, Martin 36

Mandela, Nelson 53
Martha 61, 132-138
Mary 22, 61, 132-135, 138
Maze 85
Messiah, Messianic 43, 61, 83-84, 96, 129, 146
Methodist 90, 98
Miracle 3, 134
Missionary 44, 96-97
Mob 47-55, 57, 88
Modern medicine 3-4, 74, 130
Moltmann-Wendel, E. 2, 116
Moravian 168
Mother-bird i, ii, 60, 107
Mother-in-Law (Peter's) 11-20
Muhammad 50
Mukti, Moksha, Mumukshu 26, 104

Name 34, 146-148
Narrative Theology 2
Nataraj 151
Nepal 173
New Age 4, 75, 159
Nirvana 13

Oddie N and G 174
Odic force 16
Oikos, oiko-nomy 5
Orthodox 70, 129, 167
Others (dependence on) 97-98, 105-106
Outcaste (See Dalit, Untouchable)

Parable 30
Paralysed, Paralytic, 21-30, 102-109
Peace i, iii, 5, 13, 14, 53, 67,73
Pentecost 142
Persistence 22-23
Personal, Impersonal 15, 74, 98
Peter (Simon) 11, 12, 14, 20, 35, 56, 141, 142, 143, 147, 153
Pharisees 27, 28, 43, 121, 136
Phoenix 55
Pool (Healing) 24, 102-109
Power of past 21-30
Priest(s) 38, 43
Prophetic iii, 2,6 (and passim)
Psyche, Psychological, 1, 25, 150, 166
Psycho-therapy 26, 51-52, 170-171
Publican (Tax-collector) 27, 122

Radhakrishnan, S. 114
Ramakrishna (Paramahamsa) 50
Relationship 26, 145, 159
Resurrection 7
Roman Officer (see Centurion)

Sabbath (Day of Rest)14, 57, 108, 121, 124, 125, 129
Sahi, Jane 10, 37, 173 (See also List of Poems in Contents)
Sahi, Jyoti (see Jyoti)
Sahi, Shanti i, ii
Salvation (Soteria)1, 147, 159
Samaritan 33, 91
Sanskrit 165
Satan (see also Demon,etc)
Satya Sai Baba 8
Schizophrenic 49
Scourge 3, 68-70
Seed 23, 63
Sexual(ity)17, 59-60, 69-70, 91
Shalom 73-75, 107, 130
Shaman(istic) 1, 8

Shame 69-70
Sharanam 42
Siloam 121, 124
Sishya 128
Skin cancer 5
Snowden, Rita 162
Social body 19-20, 74
Strangeness (of Jesus) 88
Subbarao 9
Suffering (Pain) i, iii, 2,6, 18, 19, 39, 40 (and Passim)
Sun of Justice ii, iii, 2, 5, 151
Synagogue 12, 14, 31, 33, 56-57
Syro-Phoenician 87-93
Swan (see Hamsa)

Tagore 154
Teachers of Law 122
Tears (Weeping) 12, 58, 133, 136-138
Temple 35, 43, 141-143
Third-world 39
Thomas, M.M. 97
Tilak, Narayan 82
Touch 38, 42, 44-46, 67-70, 75, 94, 98-99
Trauma(tic) 25, 30, 65, 117
Tree 2, 152-162
Tribal 2, 17, 80

Unexpected 24
Uniqueness 15
Upanishad 104
Untouchable (See also Dalit) 42-45, 165, 169

Vaishnava 164
Vedic 96
Violence 50-55, 59-60, 71, 116, 153
Vision 4,8, 19, 20, (and Passim)

Warning 109
Wesley, Charles 82, 158
Whittier, J.G. 14
Whole(ness) 5, 7, 9, 24, 55, 73, 85-86, 109, 125, 160-62
Wings i, ii, iii, 15-16, 23, 37, 43, 63, 107, 120, 129
Women 2, 19, 67-72, 91

Yeshua (Jesus) 1, 7
Yoga, Yogi 14, 24

Zaehner, R.C. 147